M000282342

Crocodile Tears

The Larger than Life Story of
Steve Irwin
The Crocodile Hunter

By:
Sheryl Bekstrom-Guthrie

INFINITY
PUBLISHING.COM

Copyright © 2009 by Sheryl Bekstrom-Guthrie

*All rights reserved. No part of this book shall be repro-
duced or transmitted in any form or by any means,
electronic, mechanical, magnetic, photographic including
photocopying, recording or by any information storage and
retrieval system, without prior written permission of the
publisher. No patent liability is assumed with respect to
the use of the information contained herein. Although
every precaution has been taken in the preparation of this
book, the publisher and author assume no responsibility for
errors or omissions. Neither is any liability assumed for
damages resulting from the use of the information
contained herein.*

ISBN 0-7414-5326-6

Published by:

INFIN∞ITY
PUBLISHING.COM

1094 New DeHaven Street, Suite 100
West Conshohocken, PA 19428-2713
Info@buybooksontheweb.com
www.buybooksontheweb.com
Toll-free (877) BUY BOOK
Local Phone (610) 941-9999
Fax (610) 941-9959

Printed in the United States of America

Published April 2009

"The greatest thrill is not to kill, but to let live."

J.O. Curwood

The Crocodiles Are Crying
By: Rupert McCall

Endless visions fill my head, this man as large as life
And instantly my heart mourns, for his angels and his wife
Because the way I see Steve Irwin, just put everything aside
It comes back to his family, it comes back to his pride
His animals inclusive, Crikey! Light the place with love
Shine his star with everything, he fought to rise above
The crazy man of khaki, from the day he left the pouch
Living out his dream, and in that classic Stevo crouch
Exploding forth with character, and re-defining cheek
It's one thing to be honored, as a champion, unique
It's one thing to have microphones, and spotlight cameras shoved
It's another to be taken in, and genuinely loved
But that was where he had it right, I guess he always knew
From his father's modest reptile park, and then Australia Zoo
We cringed at times, and shook our heads, but true to nature's call
There was something very "Irwin", in the make-up of us all
Yes, the more I care to think of it, the more he had it right
If your going to make a difference, make it big and make it bright
Yes, he was a lunatic, yes, he went head first
But he made the world feel happy, with his energetic burst
A world so large and loyal, that it's hard to comprehend
I doubt we truly count the warmth, until life meets an end
To count it now I say a prayer, with words of inspiration
May the spotlight shine forever, on his dream for conservation
My daughter broke the news to me, my six year old in tears
It was like she just turned old enough, to show her honest fears
I tried to make some sense of it, but whilst her dad was trying
His little girl explained it best, she said 'the crocodiles are crying'
Their best mates up in heaven now, the crocs up there are smiling
And as sure as flowers, poems and cards and memories are piling
As sure as we'll continue with the trademarks of his spiel
Of all the tributes worthy, he was rough, but he was real
As sure as 'Crikey' fills the sky, I think we'll miss you, Steve
Goodbye

TABLE OF CONTENTS

DEDICATION

I would like to dedicate this book to my children, and their children, and their children's children. The purpose of this book is to honor and remember what an incredible man Steve Irwin was and what an incredibly important mission he started, to try and secure the environment for the future inhabitants of our planet. I hope that his message remains clear.

INTRODUCTION

While writing and doing research for this book, every new sentence I wrote and every new fact I learned made me feel that much closer to Steve. I really wish that I would have written this years ago. But to be honest, I took for granted and truly believed that he was going to be around forever. Superman. The man of steel. Indestructible. Who ever would have believed that a stingray would be his kryptonite.

I am not an expert of Steve Irwin by any means. I have never done research for a book in my life. I am a fan, period. I spent years just admiring Steve and Terri Irwin and following their life from watching them on television like everyone else who loved and admired what they were doing.

On September 5, 2006, I was told by my sister (because I had not been watching the news) that Steve Irwin had been killed the day before by a stingray. It was in disbelief that I turned on the news and saw for myself that the man that had mesmerized me for so many years was really gone.

I have to admit that my feelings about it were initially very selfish and I was hurting for MY loss and then I felt guilty for my feelings. Terri...the children...they must be in more pain than anyone should ever have to endure. While I continued to hurt for me, my focus began to turn to Steve's family whom I had watched grow and flourish over the years. I began to mourn for them instead of for Steve. The family that they had always been was now broken, never to be complete again. I was also mourning for the animal world, for who else would there be that would love them as much as Steve did?

I have always been an animal lover and protector, and after Steve's passing, sent many letters to Terri and the Australia Zoo regarding a "Steve Irwin Memorial Conservation Center" to be built in California. I had never done anything like that before, so I was not surprised when my idea was rejected. However, I still felt as though I needed to be involved somehow. I just did not know what my involvement would entail. I began to self-teach by studying about animals of all sorts. From crocodiles to caterpillars, I felt an almost obsession for learning. I burned out quickly. This was not the way to go. Although it is always a good idea to learn more about anything, this was no more getting me involved than watching the Discovery Channel.

One year to the day after Steve's death, I was on my way home from taking my husband to work and I had not even heard a single word on the news regarding the anniversary of that terrible day. This really bothered me and I decided right then and there that my contribution would be a book. Having never written a book should have discouraged me, but it didn't. Not at all. I knew I could do this. This was going to be how I got involved. Before I even got home I had mapped out the book in my mind, all of the chapters and guidelines I would use. I was really going to do this and I knew from the inner peace that I got at that moment, the peace that seemed to be missing from me for an entire year, that I was doing something important and fulfilling. But how would it contribute to Steve's cause, which is what my purpose was all along? Bingo! I would donate a percentage of the profit from every book to the "Wildlife Warriors" in honor of Steve. That sounded pretty good, but not good enough. I did not ever want anyone to think that I wrote this book for selfish reasons. Bingo!!! I would donate a percentage of the profits directly to the Australia Zoo. I would also use profits to invest in other conservation efforts. Hurray! So that is what I am doing. I have a purpose and it is the animals. Helping the animals is what Steve lived (and died) for. I want to help, too.

Now, the last thing I wanted to give people was "boxers or briefs" information. I wanted to tell the world why Steve was the man he was. To do that I had to write an in-depth and revealing look into his life, childhood and the personal relationships he had with people and animals. The research involved would be extensive. I spent at least three months reading and investigating before I ever wrote one word in this book. Television was non-existent, except if there was something on about Steve. Even then, I would sit in front of the television with a notebook and pencil, taking notes on what was said. Every spare moment I had was spent writing. But my children were terrific, very understanding and supportive. They felt, as I did, that I was doing something important and they were proud to be a part of it.

The many books, web sites and documentaries that I reviewed were very helpful and informative, but most of what is written in these pages was simply from memory. What I have seen for myself and learned through the years was what kept my fingers typing everyday and the admiration I have for the entire Irwin family kept me focused.

In every chapter, I'm hoping that you find it very easy to understand and educational. I want everyone to learn that Steve was more than what was seen on the screen...so much more. To get inside his life and experiences will reveal the love he had for life, wildlife and his family. From the smallest of events as a child to life changing encounters, it was all a part of turning Steve into the greatest conservation expert in history.

Steve had done more and dedicated more to this cause than anyone else had ever even come close to doing. This is how he became the world's "Original Wildlife Warrior". Because of his efforts, many have followed suit and are doing a fantastic job. They should be saluted for their contributions, but we all need to remember that Steve was the beginning and inspiration for all of it.

Mainly for effect, I have included some facts in this book to emphasize the extreme dangers involved in some of Steve's adventures, but the primary purpose of this book is to show people that the animal world and the human world must co-exist. The environment is important to all of us. Without protection and understanding, the animal world, and hence our entire ecosystem will collapse, and us right along with it.

Of all of the possible reasons I could think of for me to write this book, the most honest and accurate would have to be that I just don't think it's possible for me to ever say goodbye to Steve. As long as I have this book, I don't have to. And neither do you. Keep him in your heart. Keep him in your mind. But most important, keep him alive by keeping his dreams of conservation alive.

CHAPTER 1

THE FIRST SIGNS OF GREATNESS

"It takes courage, strength, hope and humor to live. And these things must be bought and paid for with pain, work, prayer and tears." - *Jerome P. Fleishman*

Perhaps the best way to learn how Steve Irwin became the man that would change the entire worlds view on wildlife, is to really start at the beginning, his parents.

Steve's father, Robert Eric Irwin, was raised by his parents, Ronald and Marjorie Irwin, in the state of Victoria, Australia in the Dandenong Ranges during the depression. He is also a WWII veteran and a devoted environmentalist.

Steve's mother, Lynette Leslie Irwin, was raised by her parents, Frank and Vesta Hakainsson in Baronia and became a maternity nurse, but her true interest and passion, which soon became a lifelong mission, was caring for injured animals.

Bob and Lyn Irwin were very simple people with one very important similarity...a love for animals. It was this love that was the very foundation of their life together.

Childhood friends, Bob and Lyn fell in love as

teenagers and were married very young, at ages 20 and 18. They decided to start a family early into their marriage and soon had their oldest child, Joy. Their other two children, Steve and Mandy, would soon follow and their family was complete. At least their human family was. They had hoped, but never expected their wildlife family would grow to such a large number.

Bob is a wildlife expert and has a main interest in all things of herpetology, which is the branch of zoology concerned with the study of reptiles and amphibians. For reasons known only by him, Bob's favorite animal is the crocodile which Steve adopted as his own favorite, seeing crocodiles as beautiful and exquisite creatures in need of understanding, love and protection from those who are less educated and fearful of such a misunderstood animal.

Bob was a plumber and they owned their own plumbing business but their true passion was for wildlife. Lyn was a wildlife rehabilitator and would often take in orphaned joeys and other injured animals and nurse them back to health before releasing them back into the wild.

Lyn was a pioneer in her field. She would raise and care for orphaned kangaroos, wallabies, koalas, wombats, platypus, snakes and lizards as well as rehabilitating injured birds and other animals, while Bob would get involved with relocating crocodiles that were either in danger or considered dangerous to the local population.

Although their plumbing business was very successful, their desire to do more for wildlife and get involved in conservation and environmental issues was strong. They decided that taking care of animals whenever they could was what they needed to do.

They began taking in snakes and reptiles into their home in Essendon. After long discussions, in 1970 they decided to purchase 4 acres of land in Queensland to start a reptile park because their home was just too small to house the many animals they wanted to help. For the first couple of years after Bob and Lyn bought the property in Queensland, they had to live in a caravan because they could not build a house. Building materials were not easy to come by.

This would prove to be a challenge, having three children and themselves in such small living quarters. But everyone was willing to make the adjustment in order to do more for their cause. The children also understood how important it was to do whatever they could to help make the world a better place.

Bob had always dreamed of starting a zoo, having the same love of nature that Lyn had. It was a dream come true for both of them when after 3 years of hard work, they opened the Beerwah Reptile Park. The struggles they had and the sacrifices they made were all worth the effort they put into the park.

The admission price of the park was originally 50 cents for adults and 15 cents for children. Bob and Lyn would have to grow fruits and peppers as well as catch fish just to be able to support themselves and their children before the reptile park would begin making a profit. They had to do all of this AND run the park. During this time, they continued taking in more and more animals so the park continued to grow.

Putting all of their time and resources into running the zoo, they always knew it was the right decision and they were happy with the progress they were making every day.

The animal population continued to increase at a rapid rate. Lyn would design mock pouches for the orphaned kangaroos and other marsupials. They would have 12 or more pouches around the house, on the backs of chairs. But they were still a "reptile" park and would have snakes and lizards in any empty space they could find, both indoors and outside.

Every day the park would continue to grow larger and larger in population, and by 1980 it had grown so much it was upgraded to become the Queensland Reptile and Fauna Park.

The condition of the grounds were just as important to the Irwins as the animals, so they always made sure that the foliage and park were kept clean, healthy and beautiful.

Steven Robert Irwin came into the world on his mother's birthday, February 22, 1962. He was Australia born in Essendon, a suburb of Melbourne, Victoria. Because he shared his birthday with his mother, Steve always felt an extra special bond with her and would express this several times throughout his life.

Steve was only 8 years old when his parents bought the land and built the park that would become the Australia Zoo. It was here that Steve grew up around crocodiles and other reptiles, thus learning about and loving all the animals he would someday dedicate his life to.

Steve was involved with the park in many ways, including daily animal feedings, as well as care and maintenance activities. Large or small, he became emotionally close to every animal he came into contact with at the park. Throughout his life, Steve would often say how happy and lucky he felt about growing up at a reptile park and having the privilege of learning about and caring for the animals on a daily, then eventually, a lifelong basis.

While attending Essendon State Primary School,

Steve was not into the things that other children were doing at that age, such as skateboarding. Instead, at tea time (that's recess or lunch for all the Non-Australians out there), he would be out looking for lizards and birds or any other animal he could find under rocks, up in trees, under bushes or in the water.

His friends originally thought he was quite strange, but over time they would come with Steve to find creatures and had loads of fun doing it. They would no longer think of Steve as strange, but rather interesting, adventurous, energetic and full of life.

Steve's father, Bob, started educating him about all animals from a very early age. On his 6th birthday, before they ever bought the property in Queensland, his parents gave him a 12 foot scrub python which he lovingly named Fred. The snake was too big for Steve to play with and could have easily considered Steve a nice snack. Nevertheless, he still loved the snake and would spend time with it whenever he could, under supervision.

Bob would often take Steve with him when he went out to capture and relocate problem crocodiles. About a year after they moved to Queensland, Bob supervised Steve as he jumped his first crocodile when he was only nine years old. The freshwater crocodile that was the first that Steve jumped was a lot larger than Steve and Bob had realized, but it was too late and Steve handled it like a pro. He made the catch and Bob pulled Steve and the crocodile into the boat.

This event was probably the proudest moment in both Steve's and Bob's life. And so it began. This first encounter with crocodiles, up close and hands on, would eventually turn a man, an ordinary bloke, into a force of nature.

Bob described Steve as a boy "a monster who

was never where he was suppose to be". If they went out into the bush, the hardest part of the trip was keeping track of what Steve was doing.

Lyn described Steve as being very active, "On the verge of being hyper active…If he went missing you could always look up a tree, there he'd be". From the age of 2 years old, he would never be on the ground.

Whenever they saw a reptile while driving in the car, Steve insisted on stopping. His destiny was already apparent even at this young age, and his parents supported him every step of way. They already knew that they were raising a boy with a passionate love of all wildlife.

Although it seems at this point that Steve's parents may have been careless with their still very young son, the opposite is true. Bob and Lyn were very protective and careful with Steve and that is why they tried to educate him completely on how to conduct himself safely around the animals that he would be in constant contact with. In fact, Bob gave young Steve a swift kick in his back side for demonstrating a lack of safety concerns when Steve brought home a cooler with 7 red bellied brown snakes on a bus full of children.

The snakes are highly venomous and very deadly. These particular snakes cause the most fatalities in Australia and they are one of the most venomous snakes in the entire world, second only to the fierce snake. Bob was furious that Steve had endangered lives to bring home snakes.

On yet another occasion, Steve and Bob were out on one of their expeditions when Steve purposefully caught a brown snake with his foot and Bob quickly and forcefully knocked Steve over and kept Steve from getting bit, probably saving his life. As upset as Bob was, he used these opportunities to further educate Steve and the incidents did not re-occur. Steve was forgiven and his love affair with reptiles continued.

But this was only the beginning of a long and productive relationship that Steve would have with the animal world. Although his passion was the love and care of animals, what most people overlook was that Steve loved people. The only issue that was always a bother to Steve was ignorance. People who would kill an animal simply because they feared it, did not understand it or thought it was ugly or disgusting was wrong in Steve's eyes and very frustrating. This is what drove him to teach conservation and appreciation of all things in the environment. He also loved people so much that he wanted everyone to share in his passion and feel the euphoria he felt by protecting wildlife.

Although Steve's mission began and ended with wildlife, it was his family that his heart truly belonged to. His love for his mother and father were endearing. As far as he was concerned, the sun would rise and set in his mother's eyes and his father was nothing less than his hero, mentor and best mate.

His parents love of wildlife was the inspiration of Steve's life choices, and it was a life he adored.

Steve's passion for wildlife conservation was almost in-born. His DNA was predestined to his mission. His passion and ambition never faltered for his entire life, but only grew stronger as he grew older and wiser. The more he learned and participated in the daily care and protection of animals, the more he wanted to do for his cause.

Although it was obvious that Steve's main favor was crocodiles, he was always very interested in the largest to the smallest of creatures. Land, sea and sky, it made no difference. If it was an animal, Steve would do anything to protect and preserve it's life and habitat.

Feral animals in Australia were a threat to the ecosystem and Steve would spend countless hours trying to control the devastation it was causing.

"Feral" referrers to animals that are not native to the land. Steve always made it clear that he did not dislike these animals, he just did not want them in areas where they did not belong. He would round up feral pigs whenever he saw them. He would also go on trips specifically to track down feral camels, fox and cane toads, as they were interfering with the natural balance of certain areas. He loved the animals and knew it was not their fault, he just wanted to return them to their own environments and return the balance to the native animals.

Bob was teaching young Steve to jump and catch crocodiles in the rivers of Queensland when he was still a child. The Irwin father and son team were very proud of the fact that all of the crocodiles at the zoo were either caught with their own hands or hatched at the zoo.

Just like his father, Steve would eventually volunteer his services at the Queensland Governments East Coast Crocodile Management Program. He did this for years, living in mosquito ridden creeks and rivers in North Queensland, catching, trapping and relocating crocodiles single-handed. He loved his work and the crocodiles he would rescue and relocate. He was also adamant that they be handled as humane as possible, always without tranquilizers.

Steve's reason for not using tranquilizers was very simple. Although it would obviously make it safer for the one handling the crocodile, the use of tranquilizers would occasionally have such a negative physical effect that the crocodile would not wake up from the drug. Steve was not willing to take that kind of chance and instead would risk his own life to protect the animal. This was a philosophy that Steve would have for the rest of his life and he never once used a tranquilizer in order to catch a croc.

Because of Bob and Lyn Irwin's love of all ecological things and being naturalists by nature, it was no surprise that Steve would be every bit as involved in the cause that his parents had instilled in him since his birth. This involvement that began with the education he gained from his parent's experiences would soon become his own experiences and the centerstone of his entire life's mission.

While being involved in the reptile park was the beginning of his passion, it was his parents that were his true inspiration. Watching their love for animals combined with their dedication to each other, Steve's family values were born.

It was in the early 1980's that the decision was made by Bob and Lyn to rescue and relocate saltwater crocodiles that were considered dangerous or in danger themselves. They would either be relocated to a safer area in the wild, another river system or taken to the Irwin's Park. Injured crocs would be taken to the park and rehabilitated, then either released back into the wild or kept at the park in a suitable, lovely and appropriate habitat to live a long, happy and safe life. This is when Steve and Bob began building the Crocodile Environmental Park.

There are two different types of crocodiles in Australia. The much larger, aggressive saltwater crocodile and the less aggressive freshwater crocodile. Salties can grow in excess of 20 feet. Freshies usually do not get over 10 feet. Both types of crocodile were equally important in Steve's eyes and adored for their beauty and endurance. Steve called crocodiles "dinosaurs" because they have been around for over 65 million years and are one of the only surviving animals of the ice age.

Because they have been here for so much longer than man, Steve felt that they were deserving of the respect that they have earned over so many years. To just see them as scary killers is to not see them at all. Steve saw them for what they really were, dedicated and beautiful mothers and passionate lovers with very strong family values that are not usually present in wild animals.

It was heartbreaking for Steve to know just how crucial the situation was for crocodiles after sustaining all of these years. The numbers being so low throughout the world, Steve felt an obligation to help preserve this creature. Being misunderstood by man has pushed crocodiles to the brink of extinction and only in Australia are their numbers considered stable.

Steve loved doing research in all parts of Australia. His passion for the deserts, plains and escarpments of Central Australia was born while searching for fierce snakes in the 70's. Central Australia, or "Out West" as Steve referred to it, was about 700 miles west of the reptile park. It took around 24 hours of driving to get there from Steve's home at the zoo but he always said it was worth the drive because the beauty was indescribable and the array of wildlife was numerous. There would be many trips out west for Steve in the years to come.

Steve got his driver's license when he was 17 years old. He saved his money and at 18 years old, bought his first truck. An old yellow Toyota 4 Wheel Drive he named "Old Yella". Once in his possession, Steve drove his truck everywhere he went.

He used the truck as his home for two months while on a research trip to the Cape York Peninsula.

Setting up camp and sleeping on the ground with wild creatures all around him was second nature to Steve and it often felt more like home than sleeping in a real bed back at his house. He was always most comfortable when he felt that he was one with the nature he loved and cared for so much.

He referred to this adventure as a trip of a lifetime. The trip was to study a new breed of goanna in the rainforests of Australia. Goanna were another passion of Steve's and Australia's most common lizard.

The knowledge he learned on this trip was invaluable. But nothing ever touched him as much as crocodiles which is why he spent so much of his life trapping and relocating crocodiles. He spent more time on crocs than on any other animal.

The fact that they were so misunderstood and judged so harshly by everyone, Steve felt that he should defend them and educate people. He thought that if people would just take the time to get to know all about them, they would love crocodiles as much as he did.

Steve and Bob designed their trapping techniques in the early 1980's. The traps are designed for minimal stress for the crocodile. This was very important to Steve. The crocodiles safety and happiness was always top priority and the traps that they designed were perfect for that purpose.

The traps were made so that a "lead-in" bait would get the crocodile comfortable around the trap. After a few days of the crocodile taking this bait, Steve would put a larger piece of meat inside the trap. The bait inside the trap would be attached to a weight so when the crocodile took it, the opening of the mesh trap would gently close behind the crocodile and catch him inside without hurting him. It really was a brilliant design and one they used for most captures.

To be this careful, however, took time. Sometimes it would take all day to set up a single trap. Then it could take weeks to actually catch the crocodile. Steve would have to check the traps and re-set the lead-in baits every day. On a single adventure, with an intention of relocating 4-6 crocs, Steve could be in the bush for several months and feel that it would be worth every minute. Steve would dedicate years to save just one crocodile, his love for the animal was that strong. This was the beginning of what would become a world wide phenomenon that would last a lifetime, and longer.

CHAPTER 2
LIFE AT THE REPTILE PARK

"We must not ignore the small daily differences we can make which, over time, add up to big differences that we often cannot foresee." - *Marian Wright Edelman*

While Steve spent his entire life around animals and growing up in a wildlife park environment, life at the reptile park would be nothing less than extraordinary and completely necessary to turn Steve into the warrior for wildlife that he became.

Steve's home at the zoo was just as natural as any other childhood. When you are around animals for as long as you can remember, it is just a "normal" life. What most people would see as strange, Steve saw as just an average way of life and lifestyle.

The animals were his best friends (aside from his parents) and he could relate to them better than anyone else could. He was a natural from birth and began to understand their behaviors early on. He would spend everyday getting to know each one of the animals at the park, their routines and their behaviors, which gave him the advantage of the behavioral knowledge he obtained.

In 1985, Steve and Bob embarked on a challenge

to capture and relocate a legend.

While working for the Queensland National Parks and Wildlife Service, they were compelled to save this legendary "30 foot" crocodile that had been terrorizing the locals for 30 years or more. Working under the East Coast Crocodile Management Program, in 1988 they became the caretakers of the river system where the crocodile lived.

Bob and Steve, along with Steve's little dog, Chilli, went boldly into the river system to capture the crocodile. Bob had to return to the park for business reasons and left Steve and Chilli to capture the crocodile without him.

This capture would change Steve's life forever. Although Steve had already captured and relocated several crocodiles in his life, this one was the turning point in his career. He really bonded with the crocodile and knew that the direction he had been on was the right one for him.

The crocodile, which Steve named Acco, was indeed very large. Not the "30 feet" that had been reported but still huge. Steve tried to capture the giant crocodile by himself with his dog, but after he trapped Acco in the mesh and got him into the boat with all his strength, the boat began to sink. The crocodile was just too big for one person to handle. He still tried, though, and would use a pail to scoop water out of the boat and try to get the boat back to camp.

After Steve secured Acco, he went to a nearby homestead and recruited eight farmers to help him. It cost him ten cartons of beer, but the farmers were still scared!

The owner of some cattle property nearby also helped, using his front-end loader.

With Steve and nine other helpers, and Chilli,

they were able to get Acco into a crate for re-location. Seeing Acco as upset as he was about the entire ordeal, Steve felt guilty and wondered if he was doing the right thing. After all, Acco had lived in this river system for 30 years or more and was still alive. But then Steve heard the comments being made by the locals. Such comments as "He's so ugly" and "You should shoot the lot of 'em...". It made Steve cry. The public would not tolerate this animal and Steve knew that if he did not step in, someone was going to kill this amazing crocodilian.

Steve was worried for the welfare of Acco because he was so upset about what was going on around him and being taken from the only home he had ever known for his entire life. Not to mention being taken from his family. Steve was afraid that Acco would upset himself too much. He whispered to Acco "Please don't die" with tears coming to his eyes for the love he had for this croc.

Thankfully, Acco did not die. Steve took him to the Irwin's Park and there is were he resided in a beautiful habitat with no fear of being shot by poachers or killed out of ignorance. He also gained a new family that he loves and protects just like he would in the wild.

Acco always remained one of Steve's favorite crocodiles, even after he had obtained several more in the years that would follow.

Then there's Agro. Agro was an adventure for Steve. A very large and aggressive crocodile that Steve captured from another river system with his own two hands, with the assistance of Chilli, of course.

Agro was so powerful and aggressive, when Steve captured him and put him in a crate, he head-butt the front of the box and went straight through. One of Steve's early amateur videos show Steve catching Agro and putting him in the crate, but Agro was so aggressive that the box did not stand a chance and he went through to the other side. Luckily, Steve had set up another crate in front of that one, so Agro just went into the larger crate and was safe and uninjured.

Steve would always tell people that he and Agro had spent a lot of time together during his capture, and Agro had never forgiven him for it.

Agro was always more aggressive with Steve than he was with anyone else who would enter his enclosure. This did not bother Steve at all. He enjoyed seeing a crocodile act like a crocodile. Just as long as he knew that Agro was safe, that was good enough for Steve.

A proud Bob would often brag about his son's amazing feats but Bob's friends found it somewhat hard to believe that any one man could do what Steve did without any assistance. Frustrated and wanting proof, so to speak, Bob bought a video camera and sent it to Steve so that he could video record his captures and Bob could show his friends and prove that he was not exaggerating and his son was just as amazing as he had always proclaimed.

So, filming began long before the idea for a television show. Steve would tie the camera to a tree or set it on the seat of the boat while capturing a crocodile and soon everyone knew that Steve was in fact a phenomenon.

Occasionally, Steve would have someone else film him as he would perform the capture single handed.

Steve also realized, along with everyone else who would watch the footage, that he was a natural in front of the camera. All of this would prepare Steve for the future endeavors he did not yet know he would have.

Surfing became yet another passion of Steve's as

a kind of retreat while he was out in the wilderness. He would take a break from conservation to catch waves, then back to catch animals.

Wherever Steve was when he was saving animals or protecting natural habitats, if there were waves around Steve would grab his surf board and ride them. He brought his surf board whenever he knew that he would be in an area where he could use it.

Steve was an accomplished surfer and could ride waves that would put professional surfers to shame. Some video footage of Steve's surfing trips were also caught with the camera that Bob sent. These videos show Steve to be an incredible surfer, happy and excited with the adrenaline rush he would get when he would catch a good ride on a perfect wave.

Surfing gave Steve another outlet for all of that energy and allowed him to be physically active even during rest periods. What other people would consider exhausting, Steve called "relaxing". It also gave him a chance to be closer to nature in other ways, around aquatic animals.

* * * *

Wes Mannion was only 14 when he first visited the Irwin's park. Thrilled, he raced through the doors to see the reptiles that he had always loved and showed extreme interest in.

It was this first visit to the zoo that Wes met Lyn Irwin whom he would grow to love like a mother. She was enthusiastic to show Wes everything at the zoo and Wes could feel the love she felt towards the animals in her care. She would proceed in telling Wes everything about every reptile they would come across, and that is when Wes first saw Steve Irwin.

Wes saw a man with a crocodile that showed the same passion that he felt and no fear as he was moving the crocodile from one habitat into another enclosure. Wes thought he may be crazy to do what he was doing with such a calm about him, yet Steve was careful and so full of life.

Wes could not know how this encounter would change the entire course of his life, but that is exactly what happened. Steve and Wes would become best mates and continue to be for all time.

Wes began to spend every moment he could at the zoo. His mother would drop him off everyday in the morning and then come and pick him up later in the evening. There were never enough hours in the day and Wes would always want to stay longer than he could. He felt very much at home at the zoo with Steve and the rest of the Irwin family.

One day, when Wes was 15 years old, Steve's parents were leaving on holiday and as Steve and Wes were waving goodbye, Bob and Lyn drove out of sight. As soon as they could not be seen anymore, Steve let Wes feed a crocodile for the first time. So nervous that he was finally going to do what he had seen Steve do so many times everyday for so long, Wes did not miss a beat, like he had been doing it all of his life. Steve had trained Wes well and was very proud of how professional Wes was as he was feeding the crocodile.

Wes started working at the zoo with Steve and Steve began showing him the ropes. In the years to come, Steve would teach Wes everything there was to know about caring and protecting all wildlife, especially crocodiles, and Wes would someday be a wildlife warrior and spend his life as a conservationist and eventually, help to run the Australia Zoo.

Steve and Wes embarked on a series of adventures together, both at the zoo and in the bush. Wes proved to Steve early on that he was made of the right stuff necessary to do the work that Steve had been doing for his entire life. Although Wes did not have a lifetime to prepare like Steve did, Steve knew that Wes was a natural and would share in his passion and efforts to protect wildlife and habitats.

From the moment they met, Steve and Wes became inseparable. Sharing so much in common, Steve would eventually include Wes in almost every aspect of his life, including running the zoo and his future documentaries. Wes became part of the family, Bob and Lyn feeling the same about Wes as Steve did.

Since Steve had never had a brother, Wes was the next best thing. Steve loved his sisters, Joy and Mandy, but the bond between Steve and Wes was visible to anyone who came into contact with them and saw how well they worked together. They were always on the same page. Wes was there for Steve as a loyal brother and best friend until the very end and Steve cherished their relationship.

Wes grew up in Malaysia where his father was stationed. His father was in the Royal Australian Air Force and so Wes grew up in a jungle type atmosphere where he first had some exposure to the animals he would grow to love. Wes always had the desire to work with, care for and protect animals.

Returning to Australia in 1985, Wes was almost obsessed with wanting to visit the Beerwah Reptile Park and was elated when his mother finally took him. He was so exited when he got there, he could not even wait for his mom. He went running ahead and went inside with the excitement and curiosity of a small child.

He knew, just by watching Steve and Bob and

what they did at the zoo that it was what he wanted to do with his life. In 1988, Wes began working at the zoo full time, and in 1995 he became the manager and then later, the director. Wes had found his calling and just like Steve, it was the animals. Like he would eventually do for so many others throughout the world, Steve became Wes's hero and his mentor. Wes followed Steve everywhere, watching and learning, absorbing every new bit of information he could, and it would pay off. Wes is a wildlife expert, dedicated just as Steve was, to the care and protection of wildlife and it's habitats, as well as all thing environmental.

It was in March of 2001 that Steve saved Wes' life when Graham the crocodile grabbed Wes by his leg and Steve pulled the crocodile off Wes just in time.

It was a horrifying ordeal. During a storm, Wes and Steve went into Graham's enclosure at the zoo to clear debris from the fence so it would not cause the fence to fall when the water levels rose. They were very careful, grabbing only a little debris at a time then jumping out to check on Graham. But out of the blue, Graham snuck up behind Wes and grabbed him by the leg and backside, tearing off chunks of flesh. Steve knew immediately what had happened and grabbed Graham by the tail and pulled him away so Wes could jump out of the enclosure.

As seriously injured as Wes was, he jumped up onto the fence and turned to see if Steve needed his help with Graham. Already injured, Wes was willing to risk his own life to save Steve's.

Although Wes was pretty badly injured and had to spend quite some time in the hospital, he would make a full recovery and, thanks to Steve, live to face Graham again and again.

Wes never held any animosity toward Graham

for this attack. Like Steve, Wes knew that Graham was just being a normal crocodile and he was protecting his territory, just the way he would in the wild. It is actually a very good sign and shows that the crocodile is adjusting well in captivity.

Before this incident, Wes saved Steve's life. While Steve was giving a crocodile demonstration, he briefly turned his back on Agro and the crocodile took this opportunity and lunged at Steve, catching him off guard. Wes yelled and Steve turned, but was pinned against the fence. Just when the croc was going to let Steve have it, Wes came running toward them and briefly distracted Agro. The crocodile paused just long enough for Steve to slip away.

Occurrences like these would take place several times over the years and prove to both Wes and Steve that they could really count on each other in any time of need, no matter what. Each of them were willing to risk their own life for the other without a second thought.

In fact, Wes and Steve are not only brothers in that they were so close and had so much in common, they were brothers in spirit. They had the exact same ambitions and love of nature. Their personas were intertwined and if they were actually blood related, they would probably be identical twins! It was difficult to know where one left off and the other began. It was a beautiful friendship that not many people ever get the opportunity to experience in their lifetime. Steve and Wes were very thankful for the privilege of having such a special bond.

The physical scars that Steve showcased proudly all over his body were just the visible "dues" he paid to have such a dangerous calling in life. He also carried the burden of wanting to keep everyone else safe that was working around him. This would prove to be quite a challenge in the years to come. Whether it was in a crocodile enclosure, out in the bush or somewhere else in the outback and around the world searching for poisonous snakes or other dangerous creatures, Steve would always make sure that the people around him remained at a safe distance and that he alone was the only one in any real danger.

Steve was very proud of the fact that he had handled more venomous snakes than anyone else in the world, yet he had never been bitten by a single one. He had come close several times, though. He was, it seems, just one step ahead of the snake and it always appeared that Steve knew somehow exactly what the snake would do next. This was amazing to anyone who would see Steve handle the snakes.

On the occasions when Steve needed help with one of the crocodiles, Steve would take the "dangerous" position at the head of the crocodile and have his helpers handle safer positions like the tail or the body.

And there would be many occasions throughout the years when Steve would need help. Although Steve and Wes worked perfectly together and Wes was his best friend, Bob was always Steve's favorite helper and right hand man, or maybe Steve was Bob's, it's hard to say. Because Bob was the one who trained Steve and taught him everything he knew, Steve knew that Bob was just as cautious as he was, therefore he would worry a whole lot less. Steve knew that Bob could handle any situation that would arise, just as Steve could.

Bob felt the same about Steve. Bob said in an interview once, "If ever I am dealing with a crocodile, Steve is the one I would want by my side". Bob and Steve could catch a very large croc together and each of them would know what the other was going to do without talking about it.

Steve was so in tune with the crocodile, it was almost like he knew what the crocodile was thinking, therefore he knew what the crocodile was going to do next. This gave him an advantage over others that were handling the crocodiles.

Of course, Steve could not actually read the crocodiles thoughts, but he had been handling them for so long, he could predict what the croc may do next and then react accordingly.

In 1985 Bob and Steve felt that conflict between man and crocodiles could be resolved and began their mission to save the crocs that would otherwise be shot by hunters, either killing them out of fear, or poachers wanting them for their skins. This was indeed the true beginning of what would contribute to turning Steve Irwin into the world famous "Crocodile Hunter".

Steve would stay on a riverbank or in the bush for months to relocate a crocodile in order to save it's life, rather than give up and have it killed by someone. He would get an adrenaline rush when the crocodile was secured, just knowing that it would live a long and happy life.

Steve was in the bush for awhile when he became what he described as "a little complacent". This means that he was starting to feel too comfortable and trusting of the crocodile and letting down his guard.

He had not yet secured the crocodile that he caught and crawled into the box with his legs right by the crocs mouth. The croc bit him on the foot. Steve was lucky. He only got a bite and did not lose his leg. Seeing the video footage of this incident is really quite extraordinary. Even though you can see the crocodile chomp down right on Steve's ankle, Steve remains calm and even keeps a sense of humor about it. He says to the crocodile, "Thanks a lot!" I don't believe I've ever seen footage of Steve where he loses his composure.

Steve felt that the years he spent in the bush built him into the man he was. And indeed it was a very large part of it. The experience he gained by growing up at the park, going into the bush with Bob and the nurturing spirit of Lyn, was all contributing to the formation of a legend.

In 1991, Bob and Lyn were confident that Steve was ready to take over the reigns of the business. They retired and left Steve entirely in charge of every aspect of running the zoo and caring for it's inhabitants. Bob and Lyn continued helping and encouraging Steve in all of his endeavors, in and out of the zoo and Steve spent the rest of his life with the intentions of making his parents proud. He was successful in every way.

Steve gave demonstrations to teach people how special and beautiful crocs are and just how volatile they could be. While Steve spent so much time giving the demonstrations to thousands of people every year at the zoo and educating the public, he did not realize it at the time that the audience was actually training him for his future documentaries that would be seen by millions.

During the demonstrations, Steve would feed the crocodiles and talk about every aspect of their beauty. He would tell the audience about their mating rituals and there family structures. He would also tell about how long they have been on the planet and how that made them so special and deserving of our respect and protection.

The entire time he was talking to the zoo patrons, Steve remained so calm, no matter how close he would come to a crocodile.

The crocodile would jump at him to get a piece of meat out of Steve's hand, and Steve would stand there and continue talking like he was feeding a kitten.

These demonstrations would soon become the main attraction at the zoo, because people would be excited to see the "crocodile man" getting up close and personal with the crocodiles.

He was also successful in getting people to change their views of crocodiles. This was Steve's purpose for the demonstrations in the first place. People that went to the zoo thinking that crocodiles were ugly monsters would leave thinking that they were beautiful and interesting creatures.

Steve continued to give the demonstrations for years with great success, but he never expected that the demonstrations would someday change his life.

Steve had dedicated his life to saving wildlife and did not spend much time on socializing. He had not had many girlfriends, but little did he know that there was someone that was so much like him, his soul mate, that would be in the stands during one of his demonstrations and there was nothing he could do but let nature take it's course.

CHAPTER 3
LOVE AT FIRST SIGHT

"When we administer loving affection, it is astonishing what magical results we obtain." - *Thomas Dreier*

Anyone who is familiar with the "Steve and Terri Irwin Story" knows it's like a fairytale come true. Most people only dream of experiencing that kind of connection with someone else because it's so rare.

Terri Raines was raised in the United States, in Eugene, Oregon. She was born in 1964 and has two older sisters that are in fact much older than she is. She was raised almost like an only child as her sisters were already grown by the time she came along.

Her father ran a business that Terri became in-volved with in 1979, but she was already well business-minded. As a child she would start small business ventures of her own, such as lemonade stands, and would do very well for herself. She had a natural talent for business management and bookkeeping.

Her original involvement with animals began with her father bringing home injured animals from the roads he traveled while he was working. This became Terri's passion and in 1986 she started a rescue center called "Cougar Country" to rehabilitate and release predatory mammals such as fox, possums, raccoons, bears, bobcats and cougars back into the wild.

Her first cougar, Malina, was adopted by Terri from an ad she saw in a local paper for a cougar cub. When she went to see the animal, she noticed that it was kept in a small cage, very unhappy and in need of care. The asking price for the cat was very high, but Terri was determined to rescue this poor animal from the dreadful and neglectful conditions in which it was living. She figured out a way and came up with the money to buy her.

Malina became her pet and she would take her for walks on the beach and care for her until she was full grown. She was very close to Malina and passionate about all cougars. It did not take long before she was handling up to 300 animals a year.

Terri would take Malina to schools and functions to educate people on cougars and other predatory animals. She received a certification as a wildlife rehabilitator from the Department of Fish and Game.

Malina's favorite game was to sneak up on Terri and pounce on her from behind, grabbing the back of her neck. Malina attacked Terri one evening and Terri could have been killed. Terri learned that night that even if you raise a wild animal from a baby, no matter how much time you spend with them, they are still "wild" animals.

Having the same ideas about animals as Steve, Terri never blamed Malina for the attack and was just more careful after this incident when entering Malina's turf.

It was in 1986 that Terri bought Malina. This same year she was also running the Pilot Car business, Westates Flagman, that she had inherited from her father. Terri began working as a Veterinary Assistant in 1989 but continued working for Westates Flagman and running Cougar Country.

Life for Terri was very full and it was by pure destiny that she managed to travel to Australia in October of 1991.

A friend of Terri's was going to Australia on vacation to go scuba diving at the Great Barrier Reef and invited her along. Because her life was so busy and she personally did not like to scuba dive, she was going to decline. But then she decided that it would be a good opportunity for her to find homes for some of the cougars that she had that could not be released back into the wild.

She did not realize at the time how difficult it is to bring animals into Australia that are not native to the land. She also did not realize the extreme governmental barriers involved in such an effort.

She decided to go and it was a decision that would change the entire course of her life.

This trip with her friend, Lori, was her second visit to Australia. The first being years earlier with another old friend from school, so she already knew that she loved the country and thought it was the most beautiful place on earth.

After being in Australia for awhile with no luck, she went with her friend to the Sunshine Coast, Queensland. She saw the little sign for the reptile park and decided to take a look and see if there were any chance of arranging to have some cougars brought over.

Her expectations were low and she expected to see just a sorry little place with sad little lizards stuck in jars. But when she walked through the front entrance, she was amazed that it opened up into beautiful gardens with happy animals that were well cared for and so obviously and visibly loved.

At the zoo, there was a man doing a crocodile demonstration. Terri found him very intriguing. Steve was describing crocodiles during the demonstration as passionate lovers and beautiful mothers. Terri thought that the way Steve talked about crocs and his passion was hypnotic. She thought immediately that Steve was the most incredible man she had ever seen.

After the demonstration, Terri was first in line to buy a ticket for a tour of the Crocodile Environmental Park, listening and watching intently as Steve guided the tour and spoke endlessly of crocodiles.

Steve saw Terri in the stands and said his heart just started thumping in his chest…it was "love at first sight" as Steve put it. He almost forgot where he was, in Agro's enclosure. He wrapped up the demonstration and was hoping to have the opportunity to talk to Terri.

Fortunately for both of them, Terri was not shy about it. She walk straight over to Steve after the demonstration and both of them noticed an immediate attraction. When their eyes met, they felt like they had known each other their whole life. They began talking and Terri's friend, Lori, took a picture of Steve and Terri right at the moment they met. Terri often talks about how amazing it is to have a picture of the exact moment they met and she does not know of anyone else that has that. The chances of having a photograph of the exact moment you meet your soul mate are too rare.

Steve and Terri felt at once that they were kindred spirits, destined to be together…soul mates.

Finally, after talking for some time, they heard a horn coming from the car park and Terri realized that it was Lori letting her know it was time to go. So as she was heading in that direction to leave, Steve asked her if she would like to meet his girlfriend. Terri was devastated but cheerfully agreed to meet his "girlfriend" so Steve called Sui and introduced her to Terri. Sui was Steve's brindle Staffordshire. Yes, a dog. Terri was relieved to find out that Sui was Steve's ONLY girlfriend.

Terri volunteered her time and worked at the zoo for the weekend. She left with her friends and then went back. The weekend at the zoo, Terri spent cleaning, clearing debris and working hard. She loved every minute of it and loved how much time she was spending with Steve. Terri spent her final weekend in Australia at the zoo with Steve, getting to know him and his family as well as all of the animals.

They had dinner at a seafood restaurant called Caloundra when she spent that first weekend at the zoo. It was an all-you-can-eat seafood buffet and they filled their plates with mud crab. Terri ate so much and did not bother to be neat about it. Steve told her that she was not "lady-like" , but Steve was very happy about it. Lady-like just was not Steve's cuppa. She had the time of her life and was very upset when it was time to return home to Oregon. She could not see at this point how they would be able to continue their friendship living so far away from each other.

But neither of them would be able to stop the progression of that relationship even if they wanted to (which, of course, they did not) and Steve and Terri found a way to continue the relationship even though Terri was living in the United States and Steve remained in Australia at the zoo.

This was the beginning of the most romantic love affair in history, and there have never been two people more suited for each other. Their common interests were endless and the attraction was noticed by anyone who saw them together.

About a month after returning to Oregon and not hearing from Steve since she left Australia, the phone rang and she heard a familiar Aussie voice on the other end of the line. It was Steve and he told her that he was coming to Oregon for 10 days.

In November 1991, Steve arrived in Oregon to see Terri. During the time that Steve spent in Oregon, Terri got to show him the wildlife that he did not get to experience in Australia. Raccoons and squirrels are not animals found down under, and this was Steve's first trip to the United States. Steve was amazed and in awe to see so many animals that were new to him. Crocodiles were an everyday thing to Steve, but a squirrel was a brand new experience.

While visiting Terri in Oregon, Steve jabbed a porcupine quill into his arm "just to see what it would feel like". While Terri thought that this was a strange thing to do, she also considered it another reason to adore him, his fearless sense of adventure.

It was a wonderful 10 days, but when the time came for Steve to go home, they both felt that familiar pain that they felt when Terri left Australia. But by this time, they were in love and were determined to find a way to make it work.

In January of 1992, Terri was back in Australia. She stayed in Australia for four weeks with Steve's family in their home at the zoo.

While staying at the zoo, Terri spent a lot of time working, so Steve wanted to teach her about crocodiles. To teach her how to handle a baby crocodile without harming it, he had Terri allow a baby croc to bite her so that she could learn not to pull away and hurt the baby. She obliged and to her surprise, it did not hurt any more than a small pinch. In fact, she thought it was incredibly cute how ferocious the baby crocodile tried to be.

It was during this trip that Steve took Terri into the bush for the first time. They went to the Burdekin River about 800 miles from Brisbane. Terri watched Steve and learned exactly what he did on the rivers to catch crocodiles. As nervous as she was, she always felt safe as long as she was with Steve. She also describes it saying that she had never felt so alive.

It was during this trip into the bush that Steve whispered to Terri, asking if it was still traditional to ask a girls father first before proposing, but marriage was not brought up again on this outing.

After returning from the bush on February 2, 1992, Terri was feeling as though she must look a fright after working all day to pull down a tree by Steve's house. Steve did not think she was anything less than the most beautiful woman he had ever seen. And then he asked her to marry him. After knowing Steve for only 4 months, Terri happily said she would marry him. This was the most incredible moment of Terri's life. She knew that she loved him and wanted to marry him so it was easy to say yes. And loving Terri as much as he knew he did, it was easy for Steve to ask her.

When Lyn came outside, she knew by the way they looked what had happened and she was thrilled for them. She knew that Terri would make her son very happy and she loved Terri as well. They planned the wedding for 4 months later to be held in Terri's home town of Eugene, Oregon.

The time leading up to the wedding would be hectic for Terri. She was not only getting married, she was turning her world upside down (or upside down-under). She was going to leave her home and her family, her job and the animals that she had been taking care of for so many years. It was going to be a dramatic transition, as it would be for anyone.

Terri had to find new homes for her rescued animals in Oregon and also find someone to take over Cougar Country before she left to go live in Australia after her and Steve got married. She also had to see what needed to be done to have Malina shipped to Australia. Malina was not just her cougar, she was her baby, and Terri wanted to bring her with them to start their new life together.

But anything Terri had to do was worth it just to be with Steve. He was the love of her life and she knew that any sacrifices she made would not feel like sacrifices at all because she would be spending her life with her soul mate. She knew that Steve was her perfect match, the one she had been waiting for her entire life. She was not going to let this opportunity slip away, especially over something as small as half a world.

After whirlwind planning, Steve and Terri were married on June 4, 1992. Terri was glowing, and Steve was sweating buckets! He was so nervous, as he explained it, he had never been so scared in his entire life. Even catching a 15 foot crocodile was not as scary as getting married and he said point blank, he was only going to do that once!

But he knew that he was doing the right thing. Like Terri, Steve felt that they were kindred spirits and perfect for each other. It had taken Steve a lifetime to find someone that he wanted to share his existence with and he was not letting go. This was the real deal and in front of God and everybody, Steve vowed to love Terri forever…and he did.

It was a beautiful ceremony. Terri wore the same beautiful white wedding gown that had been worn by both of her older sisters, Bonnie and Tricia, when they were married so many years before. The wedding cake was made with real flowers rather than iced, and there were hundreds in attendance. It was, in every way, a dream come true.

Right after the wedding, Steve got a call from a film producer by the name of John Stainton in Australia who says their going to catch crocodiles and film it.

John informed Steve that there was a crocodile that was at risk of being killed by hunters and John wanted Steve to come and save it before that happened. Steve was not sure how Terri would take this news but was pleasantly surprised when Terri was all for it. Having yet another confirmation that he had found his soul mate, the day after the wedding, they were off to Cattle Creek in North Queensland to film their first documentary. What a honeymoon! Catching and relocating crocodiles was the perfect beginning of their life together.

This was yet another brand new experience for Terri. One of so many in the past months. Going with Steve in the bush was one thing, but now going out with a camera crew on her honeymoon to capture crocodiles was not just exciting to her, but terrifying in so many ways.

Maybe she was a little disappointed that she did not have the privacy with Steve on her honeymoon that she was expecting, but they found ways here and there to spend a little time alone together.

It was indeed the most un-traditional honeymoon in history, but totally appropriate and expected for anyone who knew the newlywed Irwins.

Sadly, the crocodile that they went to rescue had already been killed, but the trip was not a total waste. They were able to rescue a female crocodile in the same river system. Also, they found other filming opportunities with different wildlife in the area.

Early into their honeymoon adventure, Terri left the group to find some privacy behind a bush when she saw something shimmer and realized it was a snake. She almost sat on it and went screaming for help. Steve heard Terri's cry for help and went running toward the scream when he saw Terri running with her dunny roll (toilet paper) in hand. He saw the snake and realized that it was a very venomous black snake. Steve caught the snake, with Terri's help, and virtually saved Terri's life. This would be one of many times Steve would be her Knight in Shining Armor. Terri saw it as being so romantic that Steve had saved her life while on their honeymoon, because he came running when she yelled for help, and took the snake away from camp.

This entire scene was, of course, recorded for prosperity and when watched, appears to be quite hilarious, but I can imagine that Terri was less than amused during the event. She was, however, good humored about it and has always taken events like this in stride. She also felt safe just knowing that Steve was near by.

Terri was out catching crocodiles with Steve in no time. When they finally captured a female that they had been trying to save from poachers, Terri was really scared and nervous. But she climbed right on that 10 foot croc like a professional little croc hunter. Terri describes it as the most awesome and incredible experience of her life.

Terri was so nervous the first time she actually saw Steve jump a crocodile in the wild, but she was right there and jumped right in to help. As scared as she was, when Steve told her to help him and grab the crocodile's tail, she trusted Steve's instincts and would just grab it, without even thinking twice.

Terri was stunned, after watching and helping Steve that he use to do all of it by himself, without the assistance of herself or the film crew.

When Terri first observed Steve work so closely with the crocodiles, she was in awe. Then she was doing it as well. Surprised at her own ability to follow Steve's instructions, she just jumped right in to handle or restrain the crocs. It was a very proud moment in her life to be a part of what she now felt was such a wonderful cause as to rescue the beautiful dinosaurs.

Over the years, Steve and Terri spent half their lives together in the bush rescuing and relocating, as well as rehabilitating crocodiles and other animals in need of their help. Their passion for wildlife was almost a mirror of Bob and Lyn Irwin, a beautiful relationship, common interests and a spiritual connection.

In 2002, for their 10th anniversary, you would think that Steve and Terri would treat themselves to a second honeymoon (or first one, really). But, true to form, they spent their anniversary in Indonesia rescuing elephants.

After settling in to her new home and surroundings, Terri tried to get Malina brought over to her new home in Australia to live with them at the zoo. But it was never to be. There was too much governmental red-tape.

Fortunately, Terri was able to find a home for Malina in the states. A friend of hers owned a wildlife rescue called "Wildlife Images" in Grants Pass, Oregon and agreed to take care of Malina for Terri. One year after Terri moved Malina to her new home, Malina got sick. She was taken to a vet and given a sedative for the exam, but it was too late and she never woke up. This was incredibly heartbreaking for Terri who was already feeling homesick from time to time and felt such a loss for losing the first cougar she ever had.

It was a relief to Terri that after 9 months of quarantine, Terri's dog, Shasta, could finally come to be with her in Australia. It was a joyous occasion for both of them when they saw each other at the airport.

Another stumbling block for Steve and Terri was immigration laws in Australia. She was not an Australian just because she married one the way it works in the United States. The rules were very complicated and did not seem to make any sense at all. The regulations stated that Terri had to go back to the United States. She had to be living in the U.S. in order to be considered for residency in Australia. As Terri explained it, she had to leave in order to stay, so in December of 1992, Terri was back in Oregon.

It took a lot longer for Terri to get things situated in order to go back to Australia than she thought it would, but she used her time to visit family and friends and work for her father. She did anything she could to keep busy so she would not think about how much she missed Steve, and her home at the zoo.

Meanwhile, Steve was in Australia, filming. He was missing Terri every bit as much as Terri was missing him and he, too, was using his time wisely and keeping as busy as possible. They both knew that they would be together again soon and were counting the days.

Because they had met before ever filming The Crocodile Hunter, Steve knew that Terri loved him for who he was and not because of his fame. Terri was there, loving and supporting him, when he was just a zoo keeper at a struggling family reptile park.

Terri returned to Australia and then their life began. They went out on adventure after adventure and had fun. Steve and Terri, together, changed the name of the reptile part to Australia Zoo. They spent every moment they could together and lived their lives to the fullest. They were happy!!!

CHAPTER 4
THE CROCODILE HUNTER

"If you focus on results, you will never change. If you focus on change, you will get results." - *Jack Dixon*

"Crocodile Hunter" was only a small description of who Steve Irwin was. And even that description was misleading. When people hear the word "hunter" they think of stuffed heads mounted on a wall. Steve hunted to save and protect animals, not to kill them.

Watching the movie *Crocodile Dundee*, there is a scene when Paul Hogan's character, Mick Dundee, encounters a crocodile in the outback while with his lady friend. He kills the crocodile by stabbing it in the head. This from a man that was a self-proclaimed "Crocodile Hunter". Definitely something that Steve Irwin would never do.

Steve's purpose in filming the documentaries was that he wanted to get the public involved in his conservation efforts. He also wanted everyone to get as up-close and personal with the wildlife as he did. He thought that if he could get people involved that they would love wildlife and if they loved wildlife then they would want to save and protect it. This is why the camera was always so close to Steve and why Steve always put the animals he was talking about right up to the camera's lens, to make it seem like the animal was right there in your living room with you.

John Stainton was already an award winning filmmaker. Steve met John in the 80's when Steve would help John shoot commercials that had animals in them. Then they became close friends when John was filming a commercial with a crocodile in it in 1990. Even though it only featured Steve's legs, John was very impressed with Steve's performance in the commercial. Steve gave John the videos he had been recording of himself catching crocodiles on the rivers of Australia. John was mesmerized by the footage so much that he watched for hours, without taking a break.

John took the first film footage that Steve had given him to Mike Lattin at channel 10 Australia who aired it with huge results. The public devoured it and could not get enough. It was an instant hit.

Terri was the first to approach the Discovery Channel with the show ideas and video footage. Although the executives at the Discovery Channel were hesitant regarding the Crocodile Hunter documentaries, their subsidiary channel, Animal Planet, jumped at the chance to work with Steve. They thought that Steve was excellent in front of the camera, and the topics would be well received by both the young and the young at heart. His enthusiasm was contagious and they felt that Steve and his show was a product that they could easily sell to the public. Of course, they were right, but they could not have possibly predicted how well it would be received by viewers.

Animal Planet had only 200,000 subscribers, so they were looking for something or someone that would fare well with the viewers. A main attraction that would want the viewers to tune in regularly.

One year after they started airing The Crocodile Hunter, subscription was at an astounding seven million. In late 1996, subscriptions were at around 70 million. The subscription increases were credited to viewers signing up so they could watch Steve. Now the show is aired in more than 140 countries. The Crocodile Hunter had approximately 500 million viewers worldwide in 2006. Even now, Steve remains to be Animal Planet's main attraction and the biggest, most popular show that they air.

When the first episode of the show aired in 1992, it was an instant hit with children and adults alike. The pilot episode, filmed while Steve and Terri were suppose to be on their honeymoon, started the ball rolling with the public crying out for more. Just married and already their passion for wildlife and their compatibility was evident to the entire world.

Filming the documentaries gave Steve something that he never thought possible and accomplished more than he could have ever dreamed of, taking his conservation message to millions throughout the entire world and spreading the love of wildlife.

The shows were not just for entertainment, but for enlightenment. Education, along with research, were always Steve's main objectives.

The purpose of filming *Suburban Killers,* one of The Crocodile Hunter documentaries, was not to instill fear, but rather to educate so that people would know how to coexist with dangerous wildlife and know what to do if an accident occurred. To understand the habits of venomous snakes and other dangerous animals right in the backyards of the suburbs, man can live peacefully with them and not just rush to kill anything that they might be afraid of.

Some of the comments made by people after Steve and Terri started making the documentaries were very hurtful, from those who did not like to see others obtain success. One of the surprising criticisms came from a very well known and trusted environmental group who felt that Steve was antagonizing the animals and not helping them at all. Later statistics would prove them to be very wrong. The increase in numbers for animals that had been near the extinction list was just one example of how much good Steve had done in some of the projects he created and headed.

Because Steve performed all of the dangerous tasks himself, it made people very nervous at first to watch him jumping on deadly animals. And until the camera crew were use to him, they were afraid of filming Steve getting hurt without being able to do anything to help him.

But it did not take long for the crew to know that Steve knew exactly what he was doing and was very careful about it. Also, it did not take any time at all for the rest of the world to be on the edge of their seats, tuning in to see Steve and Terri save the animals.

Before long, every child in America, Australia and around the world wanted to BE Steve Irwin. Little boys and little girls alike. He was just like a real life superhero to them and they admired him for it.

The public responded well to Steve because he was not an actor pretending to do all of the stunts. He was real. He did all of it because that is who he really was and that is what he really did, and the public loved him for it.

The producers and backers of the show did not realize what a strong impact their documentaries would have, not just in Australia, but all over the world.

The filming of *The Crocodile Hunter goes West*

was Terri's most memorable filming experience and what she referred to as her "closest call". It happened on the way to Queensland's Simpson Desert to capture a male perentie lizard to go with the female that they already had at the park.

It was on this adventure that Steve and Terri were rock climbing down a gorge when Terri almost fell, while tied to Steve, and Steve again saved Terri's life. Although they made several climbs after this, there were never any instances or "almost" falls since this one.

Steve and Terri began working on documentaries that were filmed right at the zoo. *Sleeping with Crocodiles* was more relaxing and less lengthy. When Terri watches old tapings of this, she is amazed at what she was so afraid of back then because it is so routine now and done perfectly natural and without fear…only caution. To watch Terri then, and now, is an amazing adventure to see the transformation and so interesting to see how much she has grown since she met Steve and how much she has learned.

Steve's utmost mission was always research. Finding new ways to protect wildlife and their habitats was on Steve's mind as he woke up every morning and when he went to sleep every night. This was the inspiration for the technologically advanced program called Crocs in Space. This program was designed by Steve to monitor behaviors by attaching telemetry gear to the crocodile. This is a devise that sends information via satellite. The information is then used in an effort to reduce crocodile fatalities by studying their movements and learn when they are in areas that are inhabited by humans. Then Steve would know when a crocodile or crocodiles needed to be relocated before they are hunted and killed by either a scared individual or a poacher.

The program was very successful and has given

researchers the information they need to save countless crocodiles. This is just one of Steve's success stories for protecting the animals he loved so much.

Another success was Steve's beloved Croc One. Croc One is a boat completely designed by Steve to use for research and exploratory purposes. The boat has everything needed, not only to relocate crocodiles, but to do research as well. It has a fully equipped lab on board. It also has everything necessary to treat injured animals with medical care and is equipped to have several people on board comfortably.

One expedition that Steve and Terri embarked on was an amazing three week adventure in research.

Australia's Dingo Fence is the worlds longest man made structure, stretching more than three thousand miles. The dingo fence was originally almost five thousand miles long, but the three thousand miles that remain still make it the longest man-made structure in history.

The northern end of the dingo fence begins in Queensland, and that is where Steve started documenting this Australian wonder. It ended at the cliff-side of the Great Australian Bight, 20 days later.

The purpose of the fence is to protect sheep from the dingoes, Australia's wild dogs. But it is still unsure whether it is successful in protecting the sheep. While driving the fence line, they did not see any dingoes for most of the trip. Toward the end of the fence, they observed dingoes going over and under the fence with ease. They spotted several dingoes that had been killed by hunters. The dogs were placed on the fence, on the side in which they were shot. There were many on both sides. Maybe it can deter some of the dingoes, but the sheep are still at risk. Not to mention the dingoes that are killed in droves, by hunters and by the poisons left out to kill the dogs.

Sui was almost killed by some meat that may have contained poison, but luckily, Terri caught her in time and took the piece of meat she had before Sui ate it. Sui was watched carefully, but was just fine. It is heartbreaking to think of some of the barbaric things that man can imagine and do.

Bob once said that when Steve is dealing with animals, he only knew one way to do it...100%. This was evident in every episode of The Crocodile Hunter. Not to mention Steve's constant outgoing attitude and visible dedication.

These attributes were the foundation of the show's success and what kept it going for so long. It is also these effective methods that will keep the show on the air for many more years to come. Steve's very real feelings were evident to all who were watching. You can't fake that kind of passion, others have tried (and failed), but I won't name names. Steve was an odyssey, an original in every way.

After the show was such an obvious success, Steve started to venture in other avenues to get his message out. He made several appearances at zoos, in the United States and other countries. He also spoke at schools and gave lectures about wildlife. He did radio interviews as well and appeared on several television programs. Steve made a total of 14 appearances on "The Tonight Show" with Jay Leno over the years, making his first appearance on the show in 1999.

Steve was featured in the Wiggles DVD release *Wiggly Safari* which was set at the Australia Zoo. Steve's daughter, Bindi, was also cast in the program with a credited role. After these appearances, Steve provided his voice in an animated movie called *Happy Feet* which was not released in time for Steve to see it before his death.

Then Steve branched out in totally new territory. He decided to make a movie for the big screen. *The Crocodile Hunter: Collision Course* was a huge success at the box office and well worth the twelve hundred interviews that Steve and Terri gave while promoting the movie.

Filming the movie, Steve had to do scenes with the crocodiles without a contract with the studio because the insurance would not touch the movie when Steve insisted that he do all of the scenes with real crocodiles and never use computer images.

Only once was a fake crocodile used during filming and it was when someone else in the cast was to come into contact with a croc. But when the script called for one of the female co-stars to come into contact with a crocodile, Steve dressed like a woman and used a real croc. This was nothing less than side-splitting funny footage! This was the only part of the movie where Steve had to act like someone else. The rest of the movie he was his own natural self. The Steve Irwin we all know and love.

While he was still filming his own movie, Steve appeared briefly in Eddie Murphy's movie, *Dr. Doolittle 2*. A very funny Steve was playing himself (the only part he knew how to play) and did a small scene with Eddie that got tremendous laughs.

Collision Course won the award for "Best Family Feature Film" at the Young Artist Awards Ceremony and recognized for it's amazing footage with crocodiles.

Steve and Terri were involved in much more than just filming and caring for the zoo. They continued their quest for rehabilitation and conservation even when they were not filming or promoting.

The Irwin team captured two pair of canopy goannas and took them back to the zoo for breeding. After they hatched and were studied, Steve released them back into the wild. All of them. This was in 1993.

This particular breed of goanna is in danger and approaching the extinction list and Steve wanted to see if they would breed in captivity so that they might find a way to increase their numbers in the wild. So it was yet another successful project that was led by Steve to help the environment. The list goes on and on.

Steve was the species coordinator for large varanids throughout Australia, a position he took very seriously and was proud to be a part of. Steve would make sure that there were a viable number of perentie in captivity to sustain and maintain the numbers in the wild by breeding. Steve wrote several research papers that he had published on this subject and on their behaviors.

Steve's objective in filming The Crocodile Hunter documentaries was to bring people closer to wildlife, but also to educate and get people involved in protecting the animals that they did not yet understand. He wanted people to realize that the animals were worth protecting, re-locating and releasing.

The main focus and goal to capturing animals is to be able to safely return the animals to the wild, however, when an orphaned, sick or injured animal can not be released safely, it will be cared for at the zoo, or taken to a 2,000 acre habitat that is managed by Steve's dad, Bob, and can live safely without fear of busy roads or poachers.

After the documentaries aired, the receipts for the zoo began to skyrocket. Steve decided to include the Crocodile Environmental Park with regular zoo admission instead of charging separately.

For informational purposes, Steve took Terri to a crocodile farm and she was sickened by the inhumane way the crocs are treated there. Just learning myself about how the poor animals are raised and how much they suffer until they are murdered for their skins and meat, I cried for them.

On the way back from the horrific ordeal at the crocodile farm, Steve and Terri stopped for supplies. There was a bar next to the store. Recognizing Steve from the television show, a man began antagonizing Steve. Claiming to be a "real crocodile hunter", he explained his profession. He murdered little baby crocodiles by stabbing them in their eyes to have them stuffed and sold as souvenirs. After attempting to ignore it, Steve just could not walk away from the situation. He was just too angered by what the man was saying, and by his profession. He went back to the bar and called him out to the car park. Several of the men went out to the parking lot, and the big mouthed baby crocodile stuffer was hiding behind a larger man. Steve faced them all, ready to defend his beliefs when the men backed down and went back into the bar.

After they left, Terri noticed that Steve was crying. Steve explained that he had known people like that before and that they were evil. Seeing how strongly Steve felt about his beliefs and how he would do anything to defend them, Terri was proud to call him her husband.

Steve sustained several injuries over the years and had many scars to tell the stories of where he had been and the things that he had accomplished. From broken arms, fingers and ribs to stitches on just about every inch of his body, Steve could tell you how he got every single mark and usually a very exciting and interesting story would follow.

Animal habitat quickly became a priority for Steve the very first time he realized that the animals were running out of living space. Developers were making wildlife more and more crowded as time went by.

Steve felt that this deterioration of habitat was the biggest threat to wildlife which caused an un-balanced ecosystem. So to do what he could to remedy at least part of the problem, he purchased land in Fiji, the United States and Australia specifically to preserve habitats.

Although Steve considered all of the property he bought for habitat to be equally important, some of the land was purchased for specific purposes.

Steve and Terri purchased land in Tasmania and wanted to protect the Tasmanian Devil from becoming extinct like the thylacine, which was the Tasmanian Tiger which became extinct in the 1930's.

Steve and Terri both felt that everything was wonderful and they would remain safe as long as they were together. It was even more evident when Steve always seemed to obtain injuries only when he was somewhere without Terri. This made them both uncomfortable to be away from each other.

Filming continued for the entirety of Steve's life and the impact of the documentaries would be increasingly prosperous to the entire planet. With spin-off shows and several specials, as well as feature long programs, The Crocodile Hunter became, and continues to be a household name. Not only to describe the shows he filmed, but also to describe the man he was.

CHAPTER 5
AND BABY MAKES 3 & 4

"Every child represents a phenomenal opportunity, to help mold a leader for the future." - *David Robinson*

Steve and Terri were worried about what would happen to the zoo, the animals and wildlife conservation after they were gone. They were also worried about all of the plans that they had already put into motion toward their cause, so together they made the decision to start a family. Not just to carry on the work that they had started, but also as a living symbol of their life together and the love they had for each other. After they made this decision, they began immediately to try and conceive a baby.

Steve and Terri were in Los Angeles at the CableAce Awards. Steve had been nominated for his documentary "Ten Deadliest Snakes". He lost to Walter Kronkite but was not upset about it. He was honored to have been nominated and felt that it was more confirmation that his message was getting out there and people were responding to what he was working so hard to accomplish. Plus, he knew that Walter would be tough to beat before he even arrived that night at the awards ceremony.

Uncomfortable and feeling somewhat out of place at the after party, they decided that they would have more fun if they went to their room instead of staying around a crowd of people that they really did not have much of anything in common with. It would turn out to be a life-altering decision. They returned to their room for what Terri describes as the best seven minutes of her life. But as the old saying goes, it's not quantity, it's quality. The baby that they wanted so badly was conceived that night.

It was when Steve and Terri returned from a trip to America that Terri found out she was expecting a child. Steve was so happy, he spent hours calling everyone to tell them the great news. Terri did not even realize that Steve knew so many people, but was thrilled to realize Steve was so happy about the news that he would soon be a daddy.

Everyone that Steve told were genuinely happy for them and just knew that Steve would be an excellent father. They knew how much he loved Terri and how he protected her and thought that any offspring of theirs would be a lucky child indeed.

The Irwin's family doctor, Dr. Michaels, knew what kinds of activities and adventures that Terri was constantly involved in but told Terri that she could continue her current lifestyle. Terri trusted his advice since he had been the Irwin family doctor for so many years. With the permission from the doctor, it was off to Tasmania they went to film more footage for new documentaries. There was just no slowing them down, no matter what their future would hold.

Steve and Terri were in New Zealand to protest against whaling when Terri felt the baby move for the first time. Feeling the baby move and watching Terri's belly grow larger and larger made the whole event seem even more real and exciting for both of them.

They were sure that they were having a boy and nicknamed Terri's belly Igor. This was not what they were actually going to name the baby, but they thought it was a funny nickname for the time being.

Terri remained involved in all aspects of filming throughout her entire pregnancy when they went off to film in Tasmania. Since all of the snakes in Tasmania are venomous, Steve did not want Terri to handle them while she was in her present condition. In Tasmania, she handled a tiger snake purely out of habit. She picked it up and began talking about it to the camera. Steve was upset and scared for her but did not say a word. He had to realize that Terri was not going to just sit back and let everyone else have all of the fun just because she was pregnant. He also had to trust Terri's own instincts and believe that she would not endanger herself or their unborn baby.

Terri looked back at Steve and knew that he was upset but she was careful and nothing tragic happened so Steve let it go and tried not to be too over-protective of her. But to put Steve's mind at ease, Terri did not handle any more venomous snakes in Tasmania.

While in her third trimester, Terri went to the Galapagos Islands for the last documentary she would be able to do until after the baby came. It was to be a shark documentary shot off of the coast of Australia.

The night before Steve was to leave to film some more sharks, Terri thought her water had broke, but she did not want to worry Steve until she knew for sure. She made an appointment to see the doctor and went around lunchtime the next day.

When Terri went to the hospital, she was expect-ing to have a quick check-up then go on back home to the zoo. It was then that the nurse, amused by Terri's assumption, told Terri that she was staying at the hospital. Her water had broken as Terri first suspected and she was in labor. It was time. The baby was on it's way into the world.

Steve had driven for about two and a half hours when he got the call from Terri that she was in labor. Steve was so obviously nervous and at first, could not even find his keys. He found his keys and raced back in time for the big event...with the film crew right along with him. But Terri was not surprised and was in good spirits. She was fine with the idea of filming the birth and even airing it on the show later on.

Terri's labor was induced because her water had broken the night before and the doctor wanted the baby to be born right away. By the time Terri asked for pain medication, it was too late and they took her into the delivery room. The only thing they would give her for pain at this point was nitrous oxide, also called laughing gas, which only made her feel sick. So for pain control, she dug her nails into Steve's arm, and for reasons that only women understand, this form of pain management works very well.

Steve stayed with Terri the entire time she was in labor and coached her completely. He was patient, caring and supportive. His love for Terri and his baby that was coming into the world were obvious but his dedication was completely expected. That was just the way he was.

Steve was the perfect labor coach and encouraged Terri the entire time. He would rub her back, speak softly to her and comfort her through every painful contraction she had.

When the baby was beginning to emerge, the doctor called Steve to help deliver. He held the baby's head and eased it out, looking very enthusiastic yet comfortable with his duties. He also cut the umbilical cord right on cue.

When the doctor said it was a girl, Steve and Terri were both surprised and thrilled. Their perfect, healthy and beautiful daughter was born at 9:46pm on July 24, 1998. She weighed 6 pounds and 2 ounces.

The labor and delivery went without a single problem and Terri recovered very quickly from the ordeal.

Although they did not give much thought to girls names, expecting a boy, Steve immediately thought of the name Bindi which is the word aborigines use for "young girl" and it is also the name of one of Steve's favorite crocodiles.

Since Steve gave Bindi her first name, Terri came up with Sue after their beloved dog, Sui. Thus, Bindi Sue Irwin was here and the world was suddenly a better place.

Steve was so excited about Bindi he took her around and showed her to everyone in the hospital and was the proudest father in the world. Steve bonded with Bindi instantly and he did not even want Terri to hold her. Terri knew right then and there that she had been replaced as the love of Steve's life, and Terri could not have been happier about it. Now, they were a family.

Starting a family was the most natural thing and the most logical symbol to honor the love that Steve and Terri shared for each other. Bindi was the pride of Steve's life and Terri was aglow that she had an extension of the man that she cherished. She was beautiful and you could see instantly the heartfelt love that Steve had for his little girl. Steve was a daddy and Bindi adored him.

While Steve continued filming, Terri returned to

53

the zoo with Bindi. It was difficult to run the zoo AND care for a brand new baby. But Steve's sister, Joy, came to help with the zoo and Joy's husband, Frank, helped with the administrative end. Working part-time in the beginning, Frank would eventually work full-time and later became the general manager of the zoo. This was a tremendous help for Terri and allowed her to spend the most time possible with Bindi for bonding during those all important early months. Terri did not want to spend a single moment away from Bindi from the second she was born.

At only six days old, Bindi was off for her first filming adventure. Their first stop on their way to the United States was Double Island to do some filming of turtles. Her depute in documentaries was filmed on July 30, 1998. She was a natural little warrior.

On August 20, 1998 Bindi went to Mexico. The first overseas trip that Bindi took was successful and Bindi was truly comfortable on the road. She had her first encounter with snakes in Texas and showed obvious interest. She loved the snakes as well as any reptiles she made contact with.

Having Bindi with them while they were filming would turn into somewhat of a challenge, but everyone would happily help out. In between shoots, Steve and Terri would smother Bindi with kisses and then go back to shooting.

Terri would take whatever time she needed to nurse, and the crew were patient and understanding. Everyone loved Bindi and did not think it was a bother to have her there during filming.

Bindi soon became accustomed to filming and traveling. It seemed as though they were always on the road, flying to a new location to either film for the documentaries or to help an animal in need.

Bindi loved to fly. She had flown in a plane more than 300 times before she was 5 years old. She had a very interesting and exciting childhood. Even more so than Steve's own early years.

Steve and Terri decided that it would be best if one of them would be with Bindi all the time. If Bindi could not go on a film shoot, one of them would stay home with her while the other went on the filming trip.

Fortunately for Terri, it was usually she that stayed with Bindi and would feel bad when Steve would leave to film without them. She knew how desperately he missed them when he was gone, and Terri did not like to be away from Steve.

When Bindi returned to the zoo in time for her one month birthday, Steve was already preparing her for life at the zoo, introducing her to all of the animals. Each day Bindi would meet a new animal and she was thrilled by each new encounter.

Bindi had been introduced to every single animal at the zoo by the time she was two months old. Aside from just meeting the animals, she had touched a boa constrictor, went in with the alligators and watched countless crocodile demonstrations.

Unlike most children in the world, Bindi would have to learn much more than just staying away from hot stoves and not running with scissors. She would have to learn to live safely with wild animals around her every day.

Bindi took to the love of animals at such a young age, just like Steve did in his own youth. It was, just like Steve, the most natural and normal life and Bindi just loved how much time she got to spend with her daddy while his dream of Bindi following his lead was obviously becoming a reality.

One of Bindi's favorite animals at the zoo was

Harriet, the land tortoise. The entire family loved Harriet and she had a very interesting history.

Originally Steve and Terri thought that Harriet was a Geochelone elephantopus gutheri, a subspecies of the Galapagos Land Tortoise. Later they found out that in fact she was a G.e. porteri owned by Charles Darwin and brought to Australia in 1841. That made Harriet over 150 years old and the oldest documented land tortoise in the world.

This new information they had on Harriet just made her that much more special and the patrons at the zoo were very interested in learning more about this historic tortoise right there in Australia.

Right from the start, as soon as she could walk, Bindi was fearless. She would show instant interest in animals and reptiles (especially snakes) became her favorite.

Bindi's first intense bond with nature was at the other end of Australia at Ayers Rock. Known as Uluru, the rock is sacred to the aborigines and is the heart of Australia. Bindi approached the rock and placed her hands, and then her cheek on the rock as though she was listening to it. She stayed that way for awhile and Steve and Terri were amazed that Bindi felt the spirituality of the rock at only a year old.

It seems that Bindi was born with the same sixth sense about nature that Steve had and can often "feel" when there is a problem with one of the animals before Steve and Terri even know that it is sick or injured.

This intuition was referred to by Steve and Terri as "the force". Bindi had it and everyone knew it. This seemed to be an Irwin trait. First Bob and Lyn passed it down to Steve. Then Steve passed it down to Bindi. Although Terri was an Irwin by marriage, she was blessed with this intuition as well and hers grew stronger the more time she spent with Steve and the longer she was an Irwin.

Bindi was very strong, very early. She was holding her head up by herself at only six weeks old. She was also showing signs of being highly intelligent, with excellent hand-eye coordination.

It was on Bindi's first birthday that Steve and Terri started a new family tradition. On that day they would allow children admission to the zoo, free of charge.

There was a huge birthday cake, big enough to feed hundreds of people and everyone celebrated with them.

Bindi has such a large part of Steve in her. Steve will continue to live in Bindi and keep up all of the work that was his passion through her. Steve can be seen in Bindi's eyes, heard in Bindi's voice and felt in Bindi's passion.

One day out of the blue, Steve and Terri decided that they wanted another child. As much love as they had for Bindi and how much joy she had brought to their lives, they knew that they would love another child just as much and it would only bring them more happiness.

Wanting a boy this time, they sought the advice of experts on how to tilt the odds for having a boy. This included Terri having to completely change her diet and Steve keeping his "equipment" cool. They were both willing to make the sacrifices to reach their goal, although I think that Terri's sacrifice was greater. She would not be able to eat chocolate.

When Terri had the confirmation that she was pregnant again, she was feeling blessed all over. That familiar euphoria of knowing that she would again be having Steve's child was completely overwhelming.

With the news that he was going to be a dad again, Steve was inspired to further improve the zoo. Since the shows had aired, the crocodile demonstrations were getting more and more attention, so Steve started designs for the new arena that would hold the growing audience. Designed after the Roman coliseums, Steve would build a "Crocoseum".

One Australian summer night, the end of November 2003, Terri's water broke and sent her immediately into labor contractions. Five hours later they headed for the hospital.

On December 1, 2003, the heavens opened up and sent an angel down to earth in the form of Robert Clarence Irwin. A sweet, cute and incredibly perfect baby boy named after Steve's father, Bob, and Terri's father, Clarence.

Now Steve and Terri felt that their family was complete. Bindi loved her new baby brother. When she was first told that Robert was born and she was a big sister, she said that she was hoping for a sister but a brother was good too.

Bindi wanted to name the baby Brian. Steve told her that the baby already had a name and that it was Robert. Bindi said she would call him Brian for short, but she got use to calling him Robert and became very close to her new sibling.

Robert quickly turned into a mini Steve, copying Steve's every move and every word. He would even wrestle toy crocodiles and use all of the lingo that Steve used when he was relocating crocs. He sounded just like Steve, and looked just like Steve as he was so seriously working toward capturing the "crocodile". Steve would even set up pretend crocodiles made out of sticks so that Robert could wrestle and rope the stick crocs and feel as though he had accomplished something exciting and important. He was already in training to be a crocodile hunter. At only two years old, he was every bit a seasoned professional. An Irwin.

Robert is so intelligent, it is almost bizarre. He knew the species and names of all of the animals at the zoo before he was even two years old. This intelligence would grow stronger and soon he would be far more advanced than your average child, learning scientific terms and ecological jargon while he was still a toddler.

While Bindi's future was obviously going to be similar to Steve's, Robert appeared to be more interested in the behind-the scenes part of the business. Already showing a steady interest in the animals and conservation, Robert is comfortable having Bindi in front of the cameras while he enjoys the environmental parts of the projects.

The progress of Steve's Crocoseum was going right on task. It was turning into even more than Steve had hoped for and the grand opening was held when Robert was only 6 weeks old.

Nearby nuns had an issue with their well running dry and were desperate for help. Steve believed that if he could get the message out, then the nuns would receive enough funds to solve the problem. The opening of the arena was the perfect venue for such a cause, so Steve had planned to get help from the viewing public.

Animal Planet filmed the opening of the zoo's new Crocoseum and the opening was seen around the world. At the opening, the nuns that were receiving exposure for their plight blessed baby Robert, just as they had done with Bindi when she was the same age. It was a beautiful ceremony, and the Irwin clan were the happiest that they had ever been. But sadly, the joy and fulfillment they all felt on that day would be short-lived.

CHAPTER 6
TROUBLED WATERS

"People who think they are too big to do little things, are perhaps too little to do big things." - *Unknown*

Every life, no matter how perfect it seems, has some fallouts. Steve's was no different. He had his share of heartache and heartbreak throughout his life and he carried the pain with him until the very end.

Steve's bond with his mother, Lyn, was incredibly strong. They were very close and had a sort of psychic connection at times.

When Bob and Lyn retired and turned the reins of the zoo over to Steve, they moved to Rosedale which is about four and a half hours away from the zoo. This was not easy for Steve or his parents. Being that far away from his parents made Steve uncomfortable, so when Steve and Terri bought some property on the Great Dividing Range that was only two hours from the zoo, Steve asked his parents to manage the property. This would bring them closer together and everyone would be happier. So they thought.

The property, called Ironbark Station, was going to provide a safe habitat for wildlife, mainly Koalas, in the area that would give the animals protection from hunters, poachers and cars on the nearby roads.

Originally, the property was overrun with cattle and in very poor condition, but Steve planned on changing all of that. He began by planting eucalyptus trees, lots of them, so that the animals would have a home and food. What started out as dozens of trees would become thousands.

In February of 2000, Steve was at the zoo, planting trees and Terri was in the U.S. with Bindi. Terri was staying with her sister at a cabin they shared in Oregon and had not had any contact with Steve in a couple of days. It always made them uneasy to be out of contact with each other so they did not do it often, but this was one of those rare occasions.

One evening, while everyone was sleeping, Terri got a visit from the Red Cross informing her that she needed to call her husband at home immediately. She began to panic, but she called Australia and Steve answered the phone. This gave her some relief, but only for a moment. He was hysterical but managed to explain to Terri what had happened and why he was so upset. It was his mother, Lyn.

The family had made several trips from the old house, bringing all of Bob and Lyn's belongings to their new home. Lyn was bringing the last truckload of items to Ironbark Station, sometime around 3:00am. She was traveling with her dog to keep her company, as well as a bird eating spider in a tank.

Lyn's truck veered off the main road and hit a tree going around 60mph. It was not determined what actually caused the crash, but being as it was around 3am, it is possible to speculate that Lyn may have fallen asleep at the wheel, or perhaps she had swerved to miss hitting an animal that was crossing the road in front of her. But it will never be known for sure what happened that night.

Lyn did not survive the crash and was killed instantly. The dog was also killed leaving only the bird eating spider as the sole survivor of the accident that would crush Steve to the core and send him into such a deep and dark heartbreak.

Steve, having such a strong bond with his mother, had a strange experience at the exact moment Lyn's truck hit the tree. He knew something was wrong. For reasons he did not understand at the time, he began driving in the direction of the accident. He was headed that way when he got the call from his brother-in-law that would confirm his fear.

Steve's entire world came crashing down around him. He was living in a cloud, almost in slow motion, like nothing was real. He was lost and broken. This was by far the most painful experience of his life.

Although there would be many more heartaches and disappointments, this was the pain that was in Steve's heart that he could never shake. He just wanted his mum back. A part of Steve died that night right along with his mother and he would never get it back. His mom had taken that part of Steve's heart with her.

Terri and Bindi returned immediately from Oregon. What they came home to was unrecognizable. Their happy family, so full of life, the hopes and dreams that they would constantly talk about, it all seemed to die with Lyn. Terri knew this was going to be a hard road ahead of them and the entire family was in turmoil.

Bindi was upset as well. She cried whenever she saw Steve crying, which was often. Just when Bindi was getting to the age when she could really enjoy the time she would spend with her grandmother, that time was robbed from her and her Gran was gone.

Three months after the accident, Steve attempted to pull himself together, but in many ways was unsuccessful. He would never recover from Lyn's death, but nevertheless, he tried to regain some of his composure and went to Los Angeles to appear as though it was business as usual. His plan was to just act as though everything was fine until it was fine again, but it really did not work for him. At this point, he really thought it would never be alright again and he would never get over this loss.

Steve's show, *Croc Files,* was nominated for an Emmy Award in May of 2000, but Steve was in mourning and too upset to enjoy this achievement. Bill Nye the Science Guy won for the category. It did not seem to matter to Steve. Even if he had won, Steve had no desire to celebrate anything. As obvious as it was to his entire family and anyone who was close to Steve that something was wrong and he was not being himself, nobody else seemed to notice. I guess it can be attributed to the fact that Los Angeles is a "ME" town and nobody took the time to see that something was bothering Steve. But it would not have mattered even if somebody did reach out to him. There was nothing anybody could do for Steve that would make him feel any better or help speed up the mourning process.

It was during this trip to Los Angeles that Steve began discussing the plans for the Crocodile Hunter movie. He was desperate to ease the pain he was in and thought that if he were able to throw himself into something, anything, he could re-direct his thoughts away from the nightmare he had been living in for th past three months. If you could even call it living Surviving would probably be a more accura description of the haze he was living in during this tim

The talks for the movie began and some pla

were made before Steve was heading back to Australia.

In order to take a break from all of the pressures of Hollywood and grief as well as the demands of the zoo, Steve was inspired to take a rare break. His "holiday" would consist of 10 days in Samoa, filming a documentary on surfing. The old Steve began to re-surface in the Spring/Summer of 2000, but he would never fully recover.

* * * *

In January of 2004, Steve received another heart dart that would not only hurt but have the world examining his abilities as a parent. The whole incident was extremely over-dramatized and made me question the sanity of the entire human race.

Quickly nicknamed "The Baby Bob Incident", Steve took his 1 ½ month old son, Robert, into the crocodile enclosure. Steve fed the crocodile while holding baby Bob and all of a sudden, half of the planet had a conniption fit. The entire controversy was totally and completely ridiculous. The camera angles made it appear that Bob was much closer to the crocodile than he actually was. Bob was never in danger, but it was just bad luck that the incident occurred so soon after Michael Jackson dangled his baby out of a window. That was still on people's minds so they just put both instances into one category.

After being blessed by local nuns, just as Bindi had been, and going into the crocodile enclosure for feeding, just as Bindi did, one of the stations that had televised the event had turned the entire situation into something ugly instead of the beautifully spiritual and special event that it was. This was the beginning of the

most heartbreaking scandal that Steve could have ever imagined.

The governor-general's secretary threatened Steve, basically telling him that if he did not submit and kiss their butts, she could come and take his children away from him. This woman was obviously power-obsessed and clearly abused the power that was given to her to bully people into giving her un-earned respect. Before there was even an investigation, this woman wanted to take two happy, healthy children away from loving parents, based solely on media hype. What a lunatic!

Steve and Terri were heartbroken when child services threatened to take their children away, making accusations such as "neglect" and "endangerment".

Providing early education for his children that are being raised with wild animals is the responsible course of action. But ignorance keeps people from realizing the obvious and makes them rush to judgment regarding circumstances they are un-familiar with or do not understand.

Thankfully charges were never filed against the Irwins but there was another hurdle just around the corner. After the "Baby Bob Incident" came the "Antarctica Controversy". Yet another instance to prove that some in the media are not happy unless they are making others miserable. Well, it worked and Steve did not deserve the wrath of gossip that would follow him afterwards.

With the documentary *Icebreaker*, problems arose because it was thought that Steve got too close to the wildlife he was filming. Because international laws prohibit people from getting within 16 feet of the land animals and the waters being protected, Steve was under scrutiny for the documentary. One report even stated that Steve was riding a whale. How stupid is that!?! In the footage you can clearly see that he is in fact riding on a growler which is the name for a chunk of iceberg.

It seems that if the media could not find Steve doing anything wrong, they would just make something up. They were obviously gunning for him, the baby Bob drama still fresh on their minds.

After a full investigation that included Green Peace reviewing the film footage, it was proven conclusively that Steve did not break any international laws and at no time put any wildlife in danger. But the media frenzy had already done it's damage. Steve was crushed that people would even consider him dangerous to the wildlife he fought so fiercely to protect. To even suggest it was completely absurd to anyone and everyone who knew Steve. Even laughable. But Steve wasn't laughing. He was distraught.

No sooner did the hysterics and pain from the Antarctica issue start to ease when Steve was hit with yet another blow. His beloved dog, Sui, was diagnosed with cancer and Steve was told that there was nothing that could be done to save her. All they could do was make her as comfortable as possible until she passed away.

This was especially hard for Steve. As much as he loved all animals, Sui was more than just a pet. She had been a loyal and trustworthy friend and companion for many years. She was a member of the family.

By the time Sui was 12 years old, she had fought cancer, the loss of a lung and many other ailments throughout the years that she had survived. The Irwins had spared nothing to save their "family" member and keep her healthy and happy.

At 15 years old, Terri found that Sui was in pain and bleeding from her nose, so she took Sui to the

Veterinarian for tests and a diagnosis.

It was found that Sui's kidneys were not functioning as well as they should, but it was credited to age. Then after a CAT Scan, it was discovered, tragically, that she had a mass in her nose. More tests confirmed that the mass was cancer. There was nothing that could be done to save her. The best they could do for her was to give her sedation and pain medication as well as giving her all of the love that she had given them all of her life.

In June of 2000 Steve slept with Sui and comforted her as much as he could, but there would be nobody that would be able to comfort him. He was hurting while he held Sui in his arms as she gently drifted away.

Steve never left Sui and was distraught when she died, with Steve right by her side. Steve declared that he would not get another dog after Sui's death. He said it was just too painful.

After suffering the torture of losing his dog, Chilli, to a hunting accident so many years before, and now losing another dog he was so close to, it was almost more than he could bare. Steve realized that he just got too attached to the dogs and it was way too painful when they died. He did not think he would be able to go through this kind of pain a third time, so he just avoided it all together. He never had another dog after Sui died.

Another time that Terri was away, a tragedy occurred. The last bit of loss that Steve experienced was not only a personal loss, but a loss to the zoo, to Australia and to world history.

At 175 years old, Harriet the tortoise was the oldest recorded living creature on earth. In June of 2006, Harriet suffered a massive heart attack. Steve was told that she would not recover from the damage that her heart had sustained from the attack. Steve had to say goodbye to his oldest and dearest friend.

Steve called Terri to tell her that Harriet was going to die. Terri wanted to be with Steve during this trying ordeal and was worried about him, but she explained to Steve that Bindi did not want to see Harriet die. Bindi had been around Harriet for her entire life and wanted to remember her alive and well.

Steve understood and told Terri not to come home yet. He would not be alone to deal with the pain, but would have someone with him who had always been there.

Although Steve seemed fearless to the world that saw all of his daredevil stunts that he would perform in front of the camera, he did in fact have some fears.

As far as animals go, the only animal that Steve had ever shown or admitted to having a fear of was parrots. I guess the birds did not like him very much and he was bitten several times over the years. He would continue to do whatever was necessary to care and protect them, but there was no love-lost between Steve and these birds.

Also, since the loss of his mother in such a tragic and devastating way, Steve always had a fear of being killed in an automobile accident, but he never let any of these fears deter him from his course in life and they never slowed him down for a minute. Steve would never allow fear to stop him or even slow him down when it came to his conservation efforts and the plans he had already started on for the future. But heartache did slow him down at times when he lost someone or something that was extremely dear to him. This is when he needed someone to help him through his pain.

Wes Mannion had been there during every tragedy and heartbreak of Steve's life, including Lyn's accident, Chilli and Sui's deaths, the Baby Bob Incident, Antarctica Controversy and now, Harriet's heart attack. As always, Wes proved that he was a great friend and a great human being. Wes is the man!

CHAPTER 7
THE AUSTRALIA ZOO

"There is but one virtue---the eternal sacrifice of self." -
George Sand

Steve's dream of turning a tiny, family owned reptile park into a zoo of astronomical proportions was even more realistic than he originally thought, proving the adage that says if you can dream it, you can do it. Steve proved to all of us that dreams will come true with the right motivation and perseverance.

Filming and airing the documentaries around the globe opened up so many possibilities for the direction of the zoo, but Steve already had the visions in his head of what he wanted to do. Even years before something would be done, Steve would already have it all planned out.

Steve and Terri had agreed early on in their filming that any money they made from the documentaries would go right back into conservation efforts. They did not want the money for themselves, they only wanted to make their dreams of conservation a reality. So that is exactly what they did. When the money started pouring in, Steve would pour it right back into another conservation effort, either at the zoo, or buying property for habitat, research equipment or anything else he could think of that would benefit the animals and the environment. Not only in Australia, but in several other countries around the world, including the United States, Africa and Asia.

The expansions made at the zoo were enormous, but the other improvements were indeed remarkable. Steve did not only make improvements for the benefit of the patrons that would visit the zoo, but for the inhabitants that lived there as well.

The Crocoseum was for the benefit of both the zoo visitors and the crocodiles. It was so much bigger than the original demonstration area and could fit thousands of viewers at one time. This was good for the patrons. It was also a bigger area where the crocodiles would be and easier to travel from the habitat to the demonstration area with little stress. This was better for the animal.

While Steve would run most of the crocodile demonstrations and help with running the rest of the zoo, Terri did the paperwork and handled the business end of both running the zoo and with their documentaries. Terri was familiar with this from previous business experience when she lived in Oregon. This arrangement would work out just fine for Steve. He did not particularly like the "behind a desk" end of the business. I'm guessing it just wasn't exciting enough for him. He wanted to be moving around all the time, being physically active and always in close proximity with the animals. You just can't get that while sitting behind a desk, in an office. As active as Steve needed to be, I would bet that anytime he was indoors would have made him feel somewhat claustrophobic.

Steve had a need to spend every waking moment

doing something physical. After he could no longer use surfing as a physical outlet for all of his energy because of his problem with failing knees, he was introduced to mixed martial arts (MMA) by one of the zoo employees. He took to it instantly, enjoying the huge amounts of energy and endurance it would take. He also showed great promise in the sport , almost immediately.

Every morning Steve would spar with other employees. Anyone who wanted to give it a try, Steve would give them a shot. He was so good at it, there was not a single person at the zoo that would be able to beat him in a sparing match. Even Terri gave it a try, but I suspect that when he would spar with Terri, he may have wanted her to win!

Eventually, professional MMA fighters came to the zoo so that Steve could have a challenge and he faced them with enthusiasm. He was good, and even the professionals agreed that he could have chosen MMA as a profession and would have done very well at it. He had even trained with Greg Jackson, a well known professional in Mixed Martial Arts.

Steve only knew that he enjoyed it and it was a way for him to be physical and not miss his surfing as much. He continued practicing the sport for the rest of his life and continued to improve the longer he was involved with it.

Steve has done so much to help many animals in captivity and in the wild, but he has also discovered a new, never before documented animal in the wild. He discovered a new breed of turtle while exploring with his dad.

It was in the early 1980's when Steve spotted a turtle that he did not recognize, but was unable to catch. He thought it was an unusual turtle with a bright pink nose and he was sure that he had never seen one before.

Years later, he saw another one and this time he caught it and brought it home to the zoo with him. It was confirmed that it was indeed a species of turtle that had not yet been identified, so it was named after Steve and called Elseya Irwini or "Irwin's Turtle". Steve had re-discovered the turtle while shooting a film called *Hidden River*. He was thrilled to have discovered a new species AND have it named after him!

Steve decided to start programs that would help increase the numbers of species that were near the endangered lists, so he implemented a state of the art Endangered Species Unit, or ESU, right at the Australia Zoo. The unit is designed to mimic the needs of endangered species in the wild.

This program includes breeding in captivity and helping the canopy goannas of Far North Queensland, the critically endangered rusty monitor and the Fijian Crested Iguana. No expense has been spared to ensure the programs success. The numbers of these animals continue to increase because of this program.

There is a 24 hour care facility at the Australia Zoo to provide veterinary aid to the animals. Although it is a huge expense for the zoo, it is necessary to continue helping sick and injured animals. Not only at the zoo, but animals brought to the zoo in need of rehabilitation.

The facility employs full time veterinarians and researchers that continuously work to improve the health and conditions of wildlife. The success of this program has made it possible to ensure that every animal at the zoo is healthy, happy and striving in captivity. It has also made it possible to rehabilitate animals so that they can be safely returned to their own habitats in the wild.

Steve has been honored for his many achievements over the years by several organizations that recognize how important his work was while he was here and will continue to be as long as the programs are continued.

In 2001, Steve was awarded with the Centenary Medal for his conservation work and his contributions to Australia tourism. He was honored again in 2004 as Tourism Export of the Year.

Another nomination he received in 2004 was for Australian of the Year, but because of the controversy over the "Baby Bob Incident", it is possible that the occurrence could have tipped the scales against Steve and was the reason he lost to Cricket Captain, Steve Waugh. But maybe not. Steve Waugh is also a great Australian and he deserved the honor as well.

The University of Queensland's Integrative Biology had already decided to award Steve to be an Honorary Professor. The letter was sent to Steve of the award, but Steve was killed before returning home to see the letter from the University. He would have been overjoyed at the acknowledgement of his contributions to the field and to have even more of this type of confirmation that his message was being spread to such a large degree.

There have been several things named after Steve since his death, including the garden at Discovery Channel, Conservation Centers and streets. But perhaps what would have made Steve the proudest would be the baby gorilla named after him by the Rwanda Government as a tribute to his work in conservation and wildlife rehabilitation.

Even with all of the achievements that Steve made in his life and work, there is always the people that have a negative spin to put on things. It is surprising that even with all of the proof that everything Steve had done had a positive effect of the environment, the criticism from some made absolutely no sense. The claims they were making about Steve had already been proven to be false, yet they continued, both during his life and after his death, to minimize and even turn all of the good he did into something bad, as though he had done something wrong.

Steve's childhood hero, Jacques Cousteau, was said to be a responsible conservationist "as opposed to Steve Irwin who looks like a cheap reality TV star". These statements were obviously made by those who had not taken the time to check the facts.

Jacques Cousteau's son and grandson also differed on the subject. Jacques' son agreed, to a certain point, that Steve had pushed his boundaries and got a little bit too close to the wildlife, but his grandson, Philippe, thought that Steve was an amazing conservationist that had done more for the environment than any other conservationist in history. I bet you can guess which one I am siding with.

Despite all of the negative statements made by ignorant people, Steve always continued to push forward. The comments did not matter to him as long as HE knew that what he was doing was helping the animals. He realized that no matter what he did, there would always be those that would want to put him down for it. He would keep his eye on the prize and remember that statistics never lie. If the numbers were going up, and animals were being taken off of the threatened or endangered lists, how could some people consider that to be a bad thing? But they did.

It is still confusing, however, that the people that would put Steve down the most could do so without being informed. There criticism was also completely misplaced. While those individuals were so busy talking about how Steve was doing the wrong things with conservation, the real threats went unnoticed. For example, Steve would get "too close to wildlife" and be condemned for it. Meanwhile, an entire species would lose it's habitat because, in the name of progress, condos and strip malls would be built, leaving the wildlife with nowhere to live. The same people that were so busy condemning Steve were completely ignoring this tragedy. They were probably even living in the condos and shopping at the strip malls.

These same hypocrites would also be playing golf on a course that could have wiped out an entire species' habitat, and never think twice about it.

Some organizations that claim they want what is best for the environment, put down others that do great things for the same cause. Glory hogs for conservation. If they aren't the one's who did it, they pass judgment on the person who did, and then accuse them of interfering. Interfering!?! Hunting an animal to extinction is interfering. Destroying thousands of miles of habitat in the name of progress is interfering. Teaching everyone to love and protect everything in nature is NOT interfering! It's really quite pathetic for anyone to say that Steve did anything but greatly improve this planet.

To make matters worse, there are those who truly believe that you can save an animal by killing it. I have never been able to figure this one out, and neither did Steve. The people who are trying to convince everyone of this have never made any kind of intelligent argument to support this absurdity. There is no way they could because it is impossible to attach intelligence to something so idiotic. Anyone who thinks you can save an animal by killing it is stupid. And I don't care who is offended by my saying that. As a matter of fact, I think I'll say it again. If you think that you can save an animal by killing it, your stupid! Regardless of this, there are still thousands of people, calling themselves experts, who stand by this moronic mentality. These individuals are dangerous to the entire world.

Steve was always thinking of the safety of others. At the zoo, he would always evaluate a situation before just jumping into it. He would always rehearse, and have the staff rehearse maneuvers before attempting an objective. This is the kind of forethought that kept Steve and his helpers safe for so many years. Even the most dangerous tasks were performed to perfection because of these types of preparations and precautions.

There were always situations that would require Steve to move animals at the zoo to other habitats. With Steve describing every step of the plan, he would run through the entire event before ever coming anywhere near the animal. Because of Steve's instincts, everyone who was involved in a project would do exactly what Steve would tell them to do, when he told them to do it, and exactly how he told them to do it. Everyone trusted Steve completely.

No matter how busy Steve was with his conservation work, filming, running the zoo or doing research, he always found time for his most treasured adventure...his family. He would spend as much time with Terri, Bindi and Robert as he possibly could. He would take them with him at every opportunity. They would spend time together in the bush and then more time together while they were out filming. Even the rare occasion when Steve would take a break, he spent that time with his family as well.

Although his down time would usually be spent with animals in some way, whatever they did, they would do as a family and enjoy every minute of their time together. His family was, and would always remain, his number one priority in life. The work he did and the goals he strived toward were always with his family in mind. He wanted to make the world a better place for them, and for everyone.

Steve never knew any other way to do things. He was only able to give a hundred percent of himself into everything he did and every project he would conjure up. If it wasn't worth putting all of his effort into, then it wasn't worth doing at all. These are the philosophies that he adopted from Bob and Lyn and continued practicing for his entire life. Lucky for us.

CHAPTER 8
CROCODILE TEARS

"The meaning of life is to love, not to be loved; to give, not to get; to serve, not to be served." - *Unknown*

Nobody on earth expected the end of such a positive influence and important mission to come so quickly. On September 4, 2006, Steve Irwin met his match and unfortunately for the entire world, it was no match.

Steve professed on several occasions that he did not believe he was going to live to see his 40th birthday. Perhaps this is the reason that he seemed to always be in such a hurry to accomplish so much in as little time as possible. He was also persistently confirming with Terri that she would take care of the animals and keep the zoo running if anything were to happen to him.

Steve would work so hard to get so much done, almost frantically, and also would live life to the fullest every waking moment, eerily as though each day were his last. This was not only because he thought he would die young, but also because he believed in enjoying life and he felt so strongly of his mission that he wanted to do as much as possible, whether he lived to be forty or a hundred and forty. Although he left us way too soon,

Steve managed to fit ten lifetimes into his all too few years on this earth. He knew how to make his life meaningful and worth something more than just taking up space and wasting time.

Steve was with Terri and the children catching crocodiles and enjoying each other, but Terri had to leave to go home, taking the children with her. She had already made the arrangements to go on a trip to Tasmania to do some more research on the Tasmanian Devils contagious cancer.

Steve went with them to the airport and they all said their goodbye's to each other, never even imagining that it would be for the last time.

When Terri and the kids looked at Steve from the airplane window, he was standing on top of his truck with a note in his hand that Bindi had written to him, waving goodbye to them as they flew off, heading for home.

After arriving back at Australia Zoo and getting everything together that they would need, Terri and the children left immediately to Tasmania to investigate the Tasmanian Devils and their deadly condition. They wanted to find out the likelihood of mothers that had the cancer of passing it along to their babies or their unborn fetuses. Terri already knew that it was more than likely because the disease had already wiped out entire colonies of the animals in some areas, being one of only two contagious cancers in existence.

They brought along with them the children's teacher and the teacher's sister to help so that Terri could get as much done a possible without worrying about Bindi and Robert. Plus, Bindi could continue doing her school work while Terri was doing her research. Then the teacher's sister could occupy Robert while Bindi studied. It was a situation that would work out for everyone involved. When Terri was not working, she would spend all of her time with the children doing things together. Plus, the children loved the teacher and they all had a very close friendship, having spent so much time together during the children's lifetime, so they were considered to be part of the family.

They had a wonderful time but as always, they missed Steve and wished that he could have come on the trip with them. Unfortunately for them, he was also busy with his own commitments that he had made so long in advance.

Jacque Cousteau was Steve's childhood hero. So making a documentary with Jacque's grandson, Philippe, was a thrill and an honor for Steve. It was like a dream come true and Steve looked forward to the adventure for months before hand.

Ocean's Deadliest was being filmed at the Great Barrier Reef. Steve was at Batt Reef, off of the resort town of Port Douglas when he faced the stingray.

Because of bad weather, filming was delayed, but Steve decided to film some footage for Bindi's new show. He went in the dinghy with the film crew and left everyone else that was with him on board his boat, Croc One.

He was diving and decided to film a stingray. With cameras rolling, Steve accidentally came too close and the stingray was startled. His barb shot up and hit Steve directly in the chest. Being filmed by cameraman, Ben Cropp, witnesses that were there, as well as those who viewed the footage afterward stated that he pulled the barb out of his chest and then lost consciousness.

It has been called a "freak accident", "destiny", "just his time". Whatever the reason is, the world was not prepared to cope with such a terrible loss of a man that was so full of life that it could be felt around the globe.

Steve's accident happened at 11:00am. Although the official time of death was 12:00 noon, it was determined that Steve probably died instantly, or at least, very quickly.

He was taken to the hospital in hopes of getting medical attention and making a full recovery. Dr. Ed O'Loughlin was the physician that treated Steve when he arrived at the hospital, but he pronounced that Steve had "non-survivable injuries".

Steve always said that if someone was hurt by an animal, it was not the animals fault. Steve would not want anyone to be angry with stingrays, it was not the stingray's fault at all and if Steve were still here, he would probably blame himself and beg everyone to do what they could to help all of the ocean's wildlife, including the animal that pierced his heart. But this does not make anyone miss him any less and I know that the pain will go on for a long time to come. No one will every recover from losing such a great hero.

Terri was contacted in Tasmania while at Cradle Mountain in Lake St. Clair National Park and told of Steve's demise. Crushed and overwhelmed, she remained strong and explained to the children what had happened to their daddy. They were all crying and consoling each other, but all Terri could think about is that she wanted to get back to Steve. She needed to be with her husband.

The arrangements were made and Terri was on a private charter plane, heading home. Still in shock, she kept her wits about her and concentrated on the children. Bindi and Robert would need her now, more than they ever have before. She was the only parent they had and she would not let Steve be disappointed by letting them down now, when they needed her the most.

The Crocodile Hunter would have no new episodes filmed. It was over and the pain was just the beginning. At this point, *The Crocodile Hunter* had been on the air for years and the world had fallen in love with Steve. We had become accustomed to seeing him and looking forward to new episodes. His shows, *Croc Files* and *Crocodile Hunter Diaries* were spellbinding and became just as popular as the original series. What was there going to be now? What would we do? And it was not just us, the public. The animals would suffer the most. There had never been anyone before Steve that had such a determination and passion for protecting and preserving wildlife.

After the news broke of Steve's accident, stingrays began washing up on shores, killed by people that were angry that one had taken Steve's life. This is an oxymoron. Any fan of Steve's would know that he would be heartbroken if he knew that people were harming stingrays to avenge his death. This goes against everything Steve believed in, and anyone who practices this should be ashamed of themselves. If you are a fan of Steve, the last thing you should want to do is to un-do everything he has taught us and the examples he has set for all of us to live by.

Lets not forget the ball that Steve got rolling. I believe with all of my heart that every one of us should do what Steve would have wanted us to do, think of the animals and do whatever we can for conservation.

Every book he wrote, every paper he published and every documentary he made was always to educate people on the importance of wildlife conservation. Protecting crocodiles, or any animals, and the environment was Steve's life's work. Only his family came before wildlife.

Even as I was doing research for this book, all I

had seen and all I read leads to Steve educating on what he knows best and wanting everyone to love wildlife as he did. If he was telling a story of something that happened in his youth, he would always manage to make it a learning experience for anyone who was listening to the story and he did his best to make every lesson as exciting as possible. Even if a crocodile came within inches of eating him, he loved them dearly and always repeated and emphasized his philosophies. It's not their fault, don't be angry with the animal.

Now, after some time has passed since his death, the world will never forget the message that Steve stressed and pounded into each and every one of us. We need to protect wildlife and habitats, not only for the animals but for us. We can not survive without them and they can not survive without our help, understanding and protection. If you can not get involved in the helping and protecting of animals, you can work on tolerance. To live in harmony with wildlife is more helpful than just killing something just because you are afraid of it.

Steve said that if there was one thing that he would want to be remembered for it would be his passion and enthusiasm, conservation is his job, his life and his whole persona, the reason he was put on this earth. To put it in his own words, "If we can touch people about wildlife, then they want to save it... humans want to save things that they love...my job, my mission, the reason I have been put on this planet is to save wildlife".

It's easy to believe that Steve was most definately right. After years of watching him and seeing how much he did for conservation, anyone would agree that it was definitely his calling. How lucky he was to have been able to exercise his ambitions and take his dreams and goals so far. To know, right out the gate, what your purpose is and to be able and capable of living your life toward your goals was truly a blessing for Steve in every way possible.

The legacy that Steve would leave behind is bigger and more accomplished than others that have lived twice as long as he lived.

Steve was fearless, that is a fact and it was that fearlessness that allowed him to go that extra mile and do anything and everything that he set out to do. No matter what it cost him.

* * * *

John Stainton, Steve's producer, made the following statement to the media on the day of Steve's death :

"Today the world has lost a great wildlife icon, a passionate conservationist and one of the proudest dads on the planet. He died doing what he loved best. He left this world in a happy and peaceful state of mind. He would have said 'crocs rule!'... One problem Steve had was that he couldn't sit still for five seconds and because the weather was bad today, and for the last couple of days, he'd been like a caged lion because he hadn't really been able to do anything too much and he said 'look, I might just go off and shoot some segments'. Anything that would keep him moving and his adrenaline going, and that's what happened. And the next thing I heard on the radio was that there was a medical emergency and the little dinghy was bringing him back with the crew. Everyone tried tirelessly to revive him, to keep him alive."

But it was too late and the permanent damage

was done. There wasn't anyone who could save him. That was it. Just like that, he was gone.

The private memorial service for Steve Irwin was held right at the Australia Zoo around a campfire with only family and close friends in attendance. Everyone just sat around the fire and told stories about Steve. Remembering the greatness of their hero and comforting each other through the mourning process was helpful to all of those that were closest to Steve. It was exactly the kind of service that Steve would have chosen for himself if he could. Most of Steve's favorite memories were sitting around a campfire with the people he loved most in the world. I believe that Steve was right there with them, comforting them and telling everyone that he was alright now.

Thousands of people left flowers, cards and gifts of condolence by the front gate of the zoo after the news broke of Steve's death. There were so many fans wanting to pay their respects, the police had to enforce traffic control and informed the public that there would be a delay. Sadly, the media coverage was so intense that Terri, Bindi, Robert and Bob were not able to see all of the support that people were offering right outside the gates.

Steve's organization, Wildlife Warriors, originally called the Steve Irwin Conservation Foundation, received thousands of donations from people around the world wanting to give their support for their fallen wildlife soldier.

Sydney Harbor Bridge flew their flags at half-mast while in mourning. And they were in serious mourning, perhaps more than the rest of the world because he was a part of Australia before he was even discovered by the rest of us. He was Australia's son.

Several celebrities made comments about Steve

and expressed their deep sympathies to the Irwin family. A few that were especially touching were made by Russell Crowe, Cameron Diaz, Justin Timberlake, Jay Leno, Australian Prime Minister John Howard, Larry King and Kelly Ripa. Sir David Attenhourough had repeatedly given Steve credit for his achievements in introducing and educating the public to all things in nature and the environment.

CNN news had aired all of the details of Steve's accident reports, and memorandum, as their headline news for more than a week after it was released to the public.

Stations began to re-broadcast interviews that Steve had done in previous years, and Animal Planet began showing highlights of Steve's appearances on the day of his death. They continued by playing more than 200 clips of Steve from his Discovery Channel career.

These types of tributes continued for three solid weeks following his death and continued sporadically for months after that. The entire world was at a loss and had no idea how it would every return from this terrible tragedy.

A state funeral was offered and is a great honor, but the Irwin family declined. They felt that it would not be what Steve wanted. Steve always said that he was just an "ordinary bloke" and would not have wanted such a fuss or that type of fanfare.

The public memorial service was very different from the private service. There were 5,500 people in attendance, not counting the zoo staff. And there would have been more, much more if there was more room. Millions wanted to attend, but the arena was obviously not equipped to hold more than who was there, already filled to capacity.

Televised, it was watched by millions the world

over and would then become a memorial video that sold off the shelves instantly. I received one myself as a gift and have watched it many times, as well as watching it as it aired live on the Discovery Channel, uninterrupted and with no commercials.

It was a beautiful celebration of Steve's life and focused on the contributions he made to this world while he was in it, showing many clips of happy moments during some footage of his shows.

There was not a dry eye in the house, in the country or even the world. If you were watching, you were crying. There were several statements by friends of Steve. John Williamson sang Steve's favorite song, "True Blue", while Steve's truck was being loaded with all of the familiar equipment and drove out of the arena for it's final drive.

I watched with mixed emotions. Watching the video clips with joy and gratitude that Steve was a part of this world, even for such a short time. Then with pride as I watched Bindi with her head held so high while reminding the whole world that her daddy was a hero. The tears were falling throughout the entire service, but the most heartbreaking was to see Terri. So lost, it seemed, to be sitting there knowing that he was never coming home. Half of her, such a glorious, adventurous and fun life was now an empty hole. A memory, lots of memories were what she had to warm her heart, and her bed. I lost my composure when I saw her sitting there, watching Bindi and holding Robert, grateful that she still had these two very remarkable children, extensions of Steve, that she could hold, hug, kiss and love for the rest of her life.

On either side of Terri were reserved seats. I can only guess that they were reserved for Steve and his mother, Lyn. They were there, I know it.

Ocean's Deadliest, the documentary that Steve was filming when he was killed, was aired on January 21, 2007 on Discovery Channel. The program does not include any footage filmed on the date of Steve's death. At the end of the documentary, there is a still photograph of Steve with the message "In Memory of Steve Irwin".

It has been said that Steve is buried at the Australia Zoo. This has neither been confirmed or denied by Terri Irwin, and to be honest, I don't think it should be. I, for one, think that where he is buried should only be for the family to know. They shared him with the rest of the world during his life, they should be able to keep him to themselves now. I sincerely hope that it stays that way. I do not want to know where he is because I would never want to rob Steve's family of that privacy. I hope that everyone else can respect those wishes as well.

I was also relieved to hear Terri say in an interview in January of 2007 that the film footage of Steve's death had been destroyed.

I think Steve left this world exactly how and when he wanted to. The how, obviously, was doing something with wildlife. The when, I concluded, was before he was too old or his body was falling apart to the point where he could not spend all day, every day, doing the physically vigorous conservation work that he lived for. The thought of sitting by and watching or instructing others what to do and not being able to just jump right in and do it himself would have been torture for Steve. He would have been miserable for sure. But to miss the opportunity of seeing his children grow up would be torture at the same time, however, I believe he IS watching and is very proud of the passionate conservationists they are becoming.

Steve had already given up one of his passions,

surfing, when the doctor told him that his knees could no longer sustain that much stress. Even having to give up surfing was hard for Steve, so giving up crocodile jumping would have devastated him.

Steve's new boat was launched the winter after his death. When Bindi and Robert could not decide whether to name the boat Steve or Whale One, Terri suggested both, and so it is called Steve's Whale One.

This venture was yet another one of Steve's brilliant visions for getting people to come into close contact with whales and other ocean wildlife.

Whaling is such a waste and unprofitable, yet so many whales are killed each year that most are either threatened or endangered. Whale watching, however, is very profitable and does not harm a single whale. This was Steve's incentive for Whale One. Terri made sure that his vision for this was realized, educating people that killing whales to the point of extinction is devastating our planet for very little profit. But whale watching is a beautiful and profitable venture that will save the endangered whales and help the environment.

Crocodile Rescue Improvements at the zoo include Animal Planet's Crocodeum, Rainforest Aviary and Tiger Temple. Steve had considered expanding Australia Zoo to include other locations around the world, beginning with Las Vegas, Nevada. But these plans have not began or even been confirmed yet.

Terri is determined to carry on everything that Steve had started. She was even going to get the ball rolling on projects that Steve had not yet started on but only talked about. The plans that Steve had for the zoo that he intended to complete in the next ten years, Terri wanted it done in five. Steve's legacy was going to continue, Terri would see to it.

CHAPTER 9

DADDY'S FOOTSTEPS

"No one has ever found real, lasting happiness in being completely selfish." - *Unknown*

Bindi Sue Irwin had always shown signs that her intentions were to be a Wildlife Warrior, to do what Steve had always had the passion for. But after Steve's passing, Bindi's drive became even more obvious. She was driven and her inspiration was drawn from the fact that she wanted to make Steve proud. She has succeeded beyond anyone's expectations.

As I have always believed, it is not a tragedy to die doing something you love, and that is exactly what Steve did. Of course I see things a little differently now. A tragedy, yes, but we are not left empty handed. Bindi is every bit as passionate as Steve was and I know she will continue in that direction, exactly where Steve left off.

When Bindi was speaking of Steve at his memorial service, you could see the pride in her eyes. She was telling the world exactly how she felt and as heartbroken as she was that she had lost her father, the father she cherished more than anyone else in the world, she would not hang her head in defeat. I saw Steve that day. He was shinning through Bindi as clear as day, and I can see him every time I look at her. This is what Bindi said at the memorial service:

"My daddy was my hero. He was always there for me when I needed him. He listened to me and taught me so many things, but most of all he was fun. I know that daddy had an important job. He was working to change the world so everyone would love wildlife like he did. He built a hospital to help animals and he bought lots of land to give animals a safe place to live. He took me and my brother and my mum with him all the time. We filmed together, caught crocodiles together and loved being in the bush together. I don't want daddy's passion to ever end. I want to help endangered wildlife just like he did. He has been the best daddy in the whole world and I will miss him everyday. When I see a crocodile I will always think of him and I know that daddy made this zoo so everyone could come and learn to love all the animals. Daddy made this place his whole life and now it's our turn to help Daddy. Thank you."

This speech won Australia's T.V. moment of the year for 2006, receiving 43 percent of the votes. The touching and heartwarming acclamation also received a standing ovation from everyone who was present in the Crocoseum for the service.

Following the examples that Steve had given her came very easy for Bindi. She already knew exactly where she was going and what she was going to do with her life. The life that Steve had given her. Nothing was going to get in the way of Bindi following in Steve's footsteps.

Bindi filmed a memorial documentary called *My Daddy the Crocodile Hunter*. It was her first solo television program. This documentary aired on June 8,

2007 on Animal Planet. A one hour program, Bindi discussed her life and career plans, but mostly reminisced about her father. Bindi very delicately acknowledges her father's passing. She sings a little and shows some home movies of happy pastimes with Steve. It also served as an introduction to her new television series.

In Bindi's first formal interview since Steve's death, she said to ABC's Australian Story, "I'm trying to get across the message that don't be afraid of animals. They're put on this earth to help the environment and everything like that". She got her message across very well, in true Irwin form.

With full moral support from Steve, Bindi began filming her own show, *Bindi the Jungle Girl*, in 2006. A 26 episode series to promote conservation and environmental issues in a way that children could understand and relate to.

First aired on June 9, 2007 on Discovery Kids, it simulcast on Animal Planet and in Australia on July 18, 2007 with skits, singing, dancing and back up performers called The Crocmen.

On her show, Bindi has a treehouse that serves as a type of home base, but this is a small part of the program. Traveling around the world to film segments for her show, it was common for Bindi to go to the United States, Africa, Asia and Antarctica. Although she filmed in many countries, most of the series episodes were filmed right at the Australia Zoo.

Bindi focuses on lots of different types of animals on the show, such as Asian elephants from Sri Lanka and Thailand and lions in Africa. In the United States, she looks at elk, longhorn sheep, snakes, prairie dogs, wolves and bears. And in Australia its koalas, kangaroos, wombats, lizards, and of course, crocodiles.

Bindi stresses the importance of being kind to all wildlife. She also stresses how critical the situation is with poachers and others that intentionally harm animals to sell their skins for making belts, shoes and handbags as well as selling the meat. She often implores the necessity to avoid animal products like the ones listed and everything that was made by harming an animal. If you don't buy the products then you are doing your part to help the animals that are suffering everyday at the hands of the poachers that are murdering these animals for profit. If there is no market for these products then the poachers will stop these disgusting practices.

Even though it is illegal to poach an animal for the skins or tusks, it will continue as long as the poachers are making money on them.

Medical and dental care of animals is covered in some episodes. Bindi explains the importance of animal health and tours the Australia Zoo's Wildlife Hospital. Here the animals at the zoo are given check ups to make sure they remain healthy. Wild animals are also rehabilitated and released back into their own regions.

In the very first episode titled "Not Many Left", Bindi gives a tour of her treehouse while introducing the viewers to her many animals that stay right in the treehouse with her. Then she explains that the animals in the wild cannot survive without help.

Other episodes explore different parts of the world and the animals in those parts as well as endangered animals. Bindi interacts comfortably with all of the animals on her show while teaching the viewers that every animal deserves to be respected and protected by humans.

Directed mainly toward children, *Bindi the Jungle Girl* gives insight regarding animals and their habitats all over the world in a fun and easy to understand format that includes segments that children find very interesting and entertaining.

Bindi's show is a fast paced and fact based series that proves beyond any doubt that she is more than ready to take over where Steve left off. It is all she ever wanted to do and she is sky-rocketing in that direction. Bindi shows her viewers a very hands-on approach to animal conservation. Her techniques have Steve Irwin written all over them.

Lots of guests drop by Bindi's treehouse to share their own animal adventures. Plus, there is a segment in the show called "Bindi's Blog" when Bindi logs onto her e-mail and answers questions from viewers everywhere. She also has a segment called "Croc Facts" when her Croc Men disclose comical misinformation about crocodiles and other animals. In the segment called "Crikey", Terri discloses interesting information on whatever animal is the topic of the show.

A favorite segment of the show is entitiled "Croc Hunter Unplugged". Here, clips are shown of Steve from his show that are on the same subject as Bindi's current episode.

Steve had appeared in Bindi's show several times in early episodes. He is present in her treehouse and actively involved with filming and activities. He often would explain certain animal behavior traits and valuable information that is relevant to the show.

In more recent episodes that Bindi has filmed since Steve's death, she often refers to her father or shows clips and pictures of him, so proud of who he was and the contributions he made to this world while he was in it. But the topic of Steve's accident is never brought up.

The overall plot of the show is very similar to Steve's own program, to spread the word of conservation by educating as many people as possible of the importance of animals and all wildlife. Like Steve, Bindi is every bit the warrior for wildlife that Steve had trained her to be. She also practices the same caution around dangerous animals that her father taught her.

The show features segments of animals and con- servation advice just as Steve's show did. It is a fun and educational program, with Bindi showing all of the enthusiasm and excitement that her daddy had shown in *Crocodile Hunter*.

Although it is unfortunate that Steve died before Bindi's first episode had aired, I'm sure that Steve is watching with pride as his little girl carries on his message. On the show, Bindi always referrers to Steve in the present tense, as though he is still alive and right there with her.

Bindi had been on film shoots since she was six days old. She began appearing on television shows on a regular basis as early as two years old, so filming the show would be like second nature to her. Bindi has also been comfortable in front of the camera for as long as she can remember. She shows her energy and enthusiasm as though she were talking to friends that she has known for her entire life. She was already a professional and her attitude about the hard work involved in preparing for each episode was uplifting. She is always ready and willing to do whatever it takes to continue Steve's dream and keep it alive.

Bindi had been bonding with and learning about animals and conservation for as long as she could remember. She grew up at the Australia Zoo so she learned about wild animals just like other children learn about their pet cat or dog. She was comfortable around crocodiles and venomous snakes, never showing fear, since she was an infant. Bindi always shows the love

and concern for wildlife safety that she has been taught and exercises extreme caution when near dangerous animals.

Bindi has done several interviews since Steve's death. She has made appearances on such shows as *The Ellen DeGeneres Show*, *Late Show with David Letterman* and *Larry King Live*.

On October 11, 2006, Bindi presented an award at the Nickelodeon Australian Kids' Choice Awards, never showing that she was anything less than the Crocodile Hunter's daughter.

Terri and Bindi together host yet another television program called "Planet's Best" that shows re-runs of Animal Planet's greatest hits.

Releasing a DVD targeting children's health called *KidFitness*, Bindi sings and dances. With her are the Crocmen, her "co-stars" from her television show. She has also made an album called *Trouble in the Jungle* for the Discover Kids network.

In September of 2007, Bindi was the youngest person to appear on the cover of the Australian magazine, *New Idea*, in the 104 years of the magazines publication.

Bindi loves school. She says that her favorite subject is creative writing and her least favorite is math. She is home schooled and has become very close with her teachers over the years. She considers all of her instructors to be just like family. Her teachers are there on the set for lessons in between shoots so that Bindi is always right on track with her education.

Always the professional but still keeping her focus on the objective, Bindi donates a large percentage of all of her earnings to Wildlife Warriors, the charitable organization that was started by Steve to aid in conservation efforts. These are the same objectives that

Steve had when he first began filming his documentaries, putting funds back into conservation. It appears that Bindi has adopted these same values and wants money to help the animals more than for herself.

So what does the future hold for Bindi Irwin? My guess would be that the world will continue to see great things from this little extension of Steve.

For all of us that agree that the world has lost a great warrior for animal rights and protection, know that Steve's dream can continue forever. As long as we remember the lessons he taught us and the driving force behind his eagerness to make sure that the future of our planet is a beautiful one.

A legend can never die as long as those he taught continue his work and honor him by holding in their heart the love and admiration they have felt for him through his life and after his death. A hero lasts as long as his message was strong.

There is a little Steve Irwin in everyone who believed in him. With 500 million fans, each one doing just 2 small things for conservation will make a difference with 1 billion acts by wildlife warriors to better the world. The only thing lacking in most of us is the fearlessness that Steve wore so proudly.

Nobody will ever be able to replace Steve. He was, in every way, one of a kind. But he was determined enough to get his message out that even death could not stop him.

There are currently plans being discussed for a "Steve Irwin Day" in Australia and is also being considered around the world. There are millions of people that would love to see that happen. Already, as of January 1, 2007, Glasshouse Mountains Road which is the road that the Australia Zoo is on, is now Steve Irwin Way

Look to the future as Steve had always believed everyone should. Bindi and Robert are already on their way to leading us through the next generation of wildlife conservation. Terri is determined to continue Steve's work, and the rest of the world will never forget the lessons and memories he left us with in his all too short life.

Fight for what you believe in and never give up. The effects it will have on our world WILL be noticed and set the examples needed for the next generation. And the generation after that. Honor Steve Irwin the way he would want to be honored, by looking at the environment and making it better.

I can't remember who, but I once heard someone say that the brave don't live forever, but the cautious don't live at all. Steve Irwin...Lived.

CHAPTER 10
BE PART OF THE SOLUTION

"I wondered why somebody didn't do something. Then I realized, I am somebody." - *Unknown*

If you only stop being part of the problem, you automatically become part of the solution. However, there is so much more you can do and you will be astonished how easy it is to make a tremendous difference.

Now I'm sure that if you have read this book it is because you have interest in Steve Irwin and all of the great things he did for the planet. That being so, I'm also sure that you believe in his cause and would like to be a part of it, even if only in some small way. This chapter is to show you how little time and effort it takes to improve the environment and be a wildlife savior instead of a wildlife destroyer. I am including some respectable organizations to be involved in, but you can find many more from your local library and the internet. It is very important that you do at least some research to make sure that the organization in which you participate in is in deed a legitimate cause. Unfortunately, there are thousands of fraudulent organizations that do absolutely no good and only use people for monetary gain.

I am also including simple things you can do from your own home that will not cost you a dime or more than a minute of your time.

Many people talk of saving the world, but little do anything to actually move in that direction. If we have learned nothing else from Steve, it is that one person CAN make a difference. Are you going to be that one person in your home, your city, county or state? That's up to you, but you can do it and it will not go unnoticed by this and future generations to come.

To begin simply, I can not stress enough to recycle. Not only will you be helping the environment, you can also make money by doing so. Recycling centers will pay top dollar for aluminum and other metals, glass, paper and plastics. You should also recycle just about any electronic devices such as old televisions, computers, cell phones and stereos, as well as car parts such as radiators, batteries, tires and even entire cars. Most recycling centers pay even more money for the more you recycle. Some people make a very good living by recycling.

If the money making opportunities are not of interest to you, most cities in the United States and some in other countries have special bins for recycling purposes. All you have to do is separate your "garbage" from recyclable items and the city will recycle these materials for you. This takes no time at all and helps the environment in so many ways. You will be reducing the amount of items being put in landfills as well as helping stop the destruction of rainforests, not to mention helping reduce air pollution by reducing the need to make items out of new materials. There are just so many benefits of recycling that I can't possible talk about all of them in a single chapter.

Another way to help is to clean up your community by getting involved in a trash pick-up community partnership. If your community does not already have one, you may consider starting one yourself. It is very important for your neighborhood and parks to make sure that you put all garbage in trash receptacles. You can get your entire family involved and children love being a part of something important like this. Also, cleaning out gutters and fields keeps trash from ending up in wildlife areas, oceans and lakes, jeopardizing animals.

While camping, boating or just out for a leisurely day trip, always remember to clean up after yourself. By the time you leave, the area you were in should not show any signs that you were ever there in the first place.

By neglecting to do our part in this area, animals are dying every day because of debris in the wild. For instance, the sea turtle's natural diet is jellyfish. When people throw plastic bags into the oceans, the turtles mistake them for jellyfish and eat them. This causes them to choke. If they do not choke, because of air in the bag, the turtle is unable to dive and becomes easy prey. Not to mention they can't eat with a bag in their stomach so they starve to death. It is a very painful and sad situation that not enough people are taking seriously.

Another scenario is when the plastic hoops that hold six-pack cans together gets into our oceans. This causes so many deaths to dolphins and yet it can easily be prevented by cutting the hoops before discarding them and recycling.

Another easy thing that you can do that will help you be part of the solution is to have your pet spayed or neutered. There are millions of animals every year that are euthanized simply because nobody wants them. It is truly an epidemic that is so easily remedied, yet so many people will not do it for one reason or another.

Time and money being the biggest reasons people give, I can only say that if you see yourself responsible enough to be a pet owner, you should be responsible enough to do whatever it takes to protect your pet and help to control the pet population.

As far as the time excuse goes…it's not like anyone is asking you to actually perform the procedure yourself! You can drop off your pet before work and pick him or her up after work, which in total will take up around ten minutes of your day. Also, many veterinary hospitals and clinics are open over the weekend, so you can take them on one of your days off if you would prefer. Believe me, it will take up so much more of your time to try and find homes for the puppies or kittens that will undoubtedly come if you do not have this done.

It is very important to help control the pet population. Here is a realistic scenario. One person lets their cat have a litter of kittens, lets just say five in a single litter. They are lucky enough to find homes for all five kittens, so they think that they were responsible because none of the kittens were taken to the shelter and destroyed, right? Wrong!!! Those five kittens can produce five or more kittens each in a single litter, and each of those can do the same. Within a couple of years, your cat's litter and the chain reaction that follows, can produce hundreds of unwanted animals. Just one litter!!!!!!!

So you don't have the money, you say? There are so many organizations that offer vouchers to get your pet spayed or neutered at absolutely no cost to you. When you receive the voucher, there will be several veterinarians in your area that will except the voucher as payment in full. Problem solved, it's free. Just call your local animal shelter and they will direct you in the right path and either send you the voucher themselves or give you the name and phone number of an organization that will send you one.

One phone call. Time and money issues are put to rest. Have your pet spayed or neutered, end of discussion.

If by chance your pet happens to get pregnant before you receive your voucher, you can still be responsible by having the babies spayed or neutered before finding homes for them.

If you are looking for a pet, please consider adopting one from your local animal shelter rather than a pet store or private party. Save an animals life and they will reward you with years of love and affection.

I have only written a few ways to be part of the solution and all are easy and inexpensive or free. If you do these and nothing else, you are part of the solution, but there's more. Something else you can do is to be part of an organization that helps protect animals and the environment. Something as easy as making a few phone calls in the organization's behalf will fire you up to be involved. Passing out flyers, answering phones and volunteering will also be discussed later in this chapter. Whether it's something small or something that completely changes your life for these causes, you will feel reward at every corner. The more you do, the better you will feel about what you are doing and how you are helping in every way. When others see how easy it is to get involved, they will be inspired to help as well. Presto. Solutions.

Taking in stray animals off of the street is a huge way to get involved. These animals are victims. You must always remember that and treat them with the love, kindness and respect they deserve. If you could just take in two or three homeless animals a year, get them spayed or neutered, give them their life saving vaccinations and good nutrition and find them a loving home, you could end up saving a significant number of dogs and cats in your lifetime. Can you imagine if only a hundred people in your town did the same? There would be around three hundred less homeless animals every year in your city alone.

If you are worried that you will not be able to find homes for these animals, there are many pet rescues for just about any species to help you find homes or will even take the animal in. And if all else fails, there is still the animal shelter. If the animal has to be destroyed, at least it's not from a lack of trying or caring. Just don't turn a blind-eye and hope that the problem goes away all by itself. If you don't do something, then who will?

One of the most dangerous and destructive epidemics of world history is air pollution and the damage it does to the environment. Getting involved in the solution for this problem is one of the most simple of all that are listed in this chapter.

By simply giving your car a rest and riding a bike, walking or jogging as little as once a week would make a significant difference in air quality. It is not only good for the environment, but can make you physically healthier. By spending a day riding a bike, you are giving your body a day of cardiovascular exercise which will improve your heart health and respiratory system. The long term benefits for yourself and everyone else on the planet are invaluable.

Converting you automobile and cutting emissions to ensure that it meets the standards set forth by the Department of Motor Vehicles will also improve air quality by reducing smog. Yet another simple way to be part of the solution.

Everything listed so far are realistic goals that you can set for yourself that will not disrupt your life and make you an environmentalist, in your spare time!

Volunteering is not only an important and rewarding venture but a necessary one as well. Many organizations depend one hundred percent on volunteers and would not be able to function without them. Most organizations get very little donations so they can not hire a staff to run the business. Volunteering is the reason why millions of animals survive each year and you can be a part of it. Following are only a few ideas and leads to help get you started on your new journey into animal protection.

I think the most useful place to start your research to find the organization that is best suited for what it is you want to do would be the Wildlife Rehabilitation Information Directory at www.tc.umn.edu on the web. This website gives tons of useful information regarding wildlife. Included are ideas of what to do with injured wildlife and wildlife rehabilitation centers you can contact should you have any questions or need more information.

Another useful website would be Real Gap at www.realgap.co.uk. An organization based in the United Kingdom, it is the largest wildlife volunteering organization in the U.K. sending thousands of people every year to volunteer all over the world on numerous projects.

East Valley Wildlife Rehabilitation is a non-profit organization focused on caring for and releasing a multitude of wild animals and is run one hundred percent on the contributions of volunteers. If you would like to reach them, they are at www.eastvallywildlife.org. You can also write to them at 1612 Cindy St. Chandler, AZ

85225.

Project Wildlife is another highly respectable organization. Since 1972, they have been rehabilitating wildlife at a rate of approximately 10,000 animals per year. The web address is www.projectwildlife.org.

Global Vision International at www.gviusa.com works with many organizations to assist with conservation and humanitarian issues with a very high success rate as does the U.S. Fish and Wildlife Service at www.fws.gov. They have a volunteer's website attached to their home page that will give you all the information you will need to get involved in one of a number of projects they have to help the environment. They will assist and guide you in the direction you seek anywhere in the United States.

If your desire is to volunteer over seas, Global Crossroads Wildlife Volunteer at www.global crossroad.com provides for wildlife conservation opportunities in Africa and Asia.

Keeping on the volunteering subject, I realize that some of the organizations that are listed here are not realistic for many, but don't despair. There is most likely a similar organization that is close to your home. If you have trouble finding one, nearly every city has a Humane Society or ASPCA. These organizations need as much help as possible and every second of your time that you can give will be greatly appreciated.

Spreading the word for conservation is another great way to get involved in the cause. Just a word here and there in passing can get people thinking of their own involvement in the problems of conservation and may even spark a flame to get them involved in saving the world.

To be honest, the following makes me somewhat uncomfortable but it is very necessary. The organizations that care for wild animals and even domestic ones need a lot of help. All of the volunteers are great, but they don't pay the bills. These organizations need housing, food, veterinary facilities and medications in order to continue the work they do. The fact is, without monetary contributions, most of these facilities will close, causing the epidemic to grow tremendously. If you are able, please make a cash donation whenever it is within your budget to do so. It will be tax deductible and will save lives.

Supporting zoos and conservation centers is a fun way to get the entire family involved. By just going to the zoo, you are supporting the conservation of many animals by just visiting them. Without even trying, you can also find yourself being educated on all kinds of wild animals, both endangered and not. From the endangered tiger to the un-endangered camel. To a variety of birds to the giant elephant. You can learn the mating habits and the important practice of captive breeding programs in order to increase the number of certain animals in the wild.

Most zoos and aquariums offer membership opportunities. By becoming a member you can receive monthly newsletters, periodicals, or magazines and annual passes while helping the zoo continue receiving the necessary funds to continue operating. The higher status of membership that you choose, the more benefits you will enjoy. This can actually save you money depending on how often you go to the zoo or aquarium.

Most zoos and aquariums often have an "Adopt an Animal" program were you can actually choose the animal in which you wish your donations to support. This program is very rewarding because you can actually know and visit the exact animal in which you are helping to support.

Are you starting to understand how very easy it is to be part of the solution? I'm sure your getting the picture.

Earlier in this book I mentioned an organization started by Steve and Terri Irwin called "Wildlife Warriors". Established in 2002, the organization's purpose has always been to include and involve others to support the protection of injured, threatened or endangered wildlife. Best of all, there are several ways to get involved and easy enough for anyone to become a "Wildlife Warrior".

The Warrior's objectives are:

- To protect and enhance the natural environment.
- To provide information and education to the public and raise awareness of wildlife issues.
- To undertake biological research.
- To research, recommend and act in the protection of threatened or endangered species.
- To enter into cooperative arrangements with like-minded organizations.

The programs and projects that this organization started and remains active in are world renowned. Some of the projects have even raised the number of endangered animals in captivity and in the wild, saving the species. Some projects are:

- The Australian Wildlife Hospital.
- Species and habitat conservation in Asia.
- Crocodile Rescue and Research (International).
- Community Education (International).
- Emergency Wildlife Response.

Although Terri Irwin remains actively involved,

the charity is now independently operated and depends on warriors to continue it's success.

If you would like more information on how to get involved and become a "Wildlife Warrior", you can reach their website through the Australia Zoo's site or contact them directly. They are now based in Eugene, Oregon.

Since I brought up the Australia Zoo's website, I will mention that it is full of ways to get involved in many, many areas and also has links to other organizations that you can easily get involved with to make your mark on the conservation world.

Making purchases that contribute to conservation is an invaluable way to help these causes. In fact, if you have purchased this book, you have made a contribution to wildlife conservation. And just so you know, this book was printed on one hundred percent recycled paper!

Off the top of my head, I can think of a couple of other purchases that will contribute to Steve's causes. All of the proceeds from the sale of Steve's Memorial Service DVD will go right back into conservation. Also, the Wildlife Warriors wristband sales will go directly into their mission, and wearing the wristband will let everyone know that you are part of the solution.

Many websites have items that you can order that give a certain percent of purchases to wildlife and conservation causes. Please investigate before you buy to make sure it is a legitimate cause in which you wish to contribute.

Onto another area of concern, water pollution effects everyone. If local water supplies are tainted, everyone can suffer irreversible damages. Anyone can help in this problem with no effort at all.

So very important and most always overlooked…please, please dispose of unused and expired medications in the proper locations. Although it has been done for so many years, flushing these medications down the toilet can taint local water supplies, oceans, lakes and streams, causing scary risks for everyone who depends on that particular water source. There are many locations that you can take your medications to and have them disposed of properly. Most hospitals will dispose of these drugs in a safe and effective way, without jeopardizing anything or anyone. Also, hazardous waste disposal centers will dispose these items for you. Both of these places provide this service at absolutely no cost to you.

Saving water is almost as important as maintaining a healthy water supply, and there are several ways to do this.

By only watering your lawn at specific times of the day (usually during the late afternoon or evening) you can contribute in reducing water shortages. Having a sprinkler timer can avoid over watering your lawn and save even more water.

Also, nobody needs to wash their car every day. Think of how much water you can save by washing your car only once per week. If this is too much of a cut down, then wash it twice a week.

Never, ever leave your water running in the shower while your "getting ready" to get in. Get ready for your shower, then when you turn the water on, all you have to do is just step in and shower.

While on the subject of showers, nobody appreciates an hour long shower more that I do, but you really should try to keep a shower under 15 minutes.

By installing "Low-Flow" shower heads, you can reduce water usage without any kind of sacrifice at all. These shower heads are inexpensive and very easy to install. They can be found at just about any home improvement store, such as Lowes, Home Depot and Ace Hardware. Low-Flow toilets are also available.

One idea that is so often ignored or overlooked is in regards to the uses of rainwater. Rain can be collected and used for so many things, yet most people just let it fall, then forget about it.

Collect rain and use it for washing the dog or watering all of the indoor plants in your home. You can also use it to fill up your fish aquariums or for washing your clothes. I bet you have never thought to put rain into a water purifier and drinking it. Be creative and use it as often as possible. It's free and will save you money on your monthly water bills. To save money while saving water, it's a win-win situation.

This next suggestion is somewhat disgusting, so I'm sorry. If it's pee, let it be. If it's brown, flush it down. I know and completely understand if you can not bring yourself to follow this advice, but if you can, it will save an astonishing amount of water every year in one home alone. This is easier to do with less people in the home.

If you are telling yourself that it would be gross to just let pee sit in your toilet, or maybe that it's unsanitary, your right. However, unless you scrub your toilet after each use with bleach, your toilet is already unsanitary. So don't drink out of the toilet!

There are many things going on in the world that are causing a destruction of our planet that have catastrophic consequences, such as global warming, but there is little that can be done to completely stop them. From off-shore drilling to the use of certain everyday products, the environment is suffering irreversible damage and they must be addressed. Although there is no way to stop this, we can all get involved in the effort to slow it down. And maybe, just maybe if the word gets spread long enough and passionately enough, the next generation will try a little harder. And then the generation after that...and so on. If this happens, it is possible for the damages that have already been done to begin to reverse themselves. Heal themselves.

Sadly, the animals that are already extinct are gone for good, probably. With DNA and cloning, it's hard to say and we certainly can not depend on that. There is no going back and undoing that harm, but we can take whatever measures necessary to learn from the past and make sure that no other animals become extinct.

With thousands of animals on the endangered list, you can pick one, any one, and begin your journey to protect it. Try pushing for harsher punishments for those poaching these animals. Write to congress, if you can. Spread awareness. Employ to others to get involved. Whatever you do to help, you will be doing just that...helping!

The destruction of rainforests can be minimized by recycling. The ozone can be spared by not using aerosols that are damaging it. Habitats being destroyed can be reduced by not building strip malls where land turtles live. The lists can go on forever and although one person can make a difference, the more that get involved the more positive results there will be. The question is, how badly do you want the planet to remain healthy? How important do you believe it is for this and future generations for there to be clean water, clean air and animal well-being?

The next issue I would like to address at this time is the importance of "Going Green". If you don't know what this means, I will explain.

When you go to the grocery store or department

store, it is not common to look at the ingredients lists to make sure that they are made with all natural ingredients, with no chemicals, all organic. When you go green, it will become second nature to make sure you are purchasing locally grown produce and not purchasing animal tested products. Environmentally friendly products can reduce so many dangers to the planet and anything you wish to buy will also come in an all natural variety.

Green Works™ is only one company that has a variety of products that are good for the environment. If you are looking for cleaning products without harmful chemicals that still kill germs, Green Works is just the product you've been waiting for.

When you go to buy groceries, make sure to avoid plastic bags that will end up in landfills, forever. You can either recycle the bags yourself, using them again and again, or you can return them to the store and the store will reuse them. The same goes with paper bags. You can reuse them or use them for other purposes such as wrapping boxes for shipping. This comes in real handy at Christmas time. Instead of purchasing packaging materials, you can just use the bags that you have been saving for just such an occasion.

A lot of stores are now offering bags for purchase that can be used over and over so that when the clerk says "paper or plastic" you can say "neither!".

Looking for locally grown produce is great for two reasons. First, you will get fresher produce that has not traveled across the country before it gets to you. Second, you will be helping reduce air pollution because there is less fuel needed to ship the produce to your local stores.

Then there are the benefits of growing your own

produce. Gardening is a simple and relaxing activity that can be enjoyed by anyone, regardless of age or gender. There are no special skills required and will make you feel better while helping the environment. It will also save you money by not having to buy tomatoes, lettuce, carrots or whatever it is you wish to grow. You can also rest assured knowing that your veggies have not been sprayed with harmful chemicals. This is yet another win-win situation.

While we are on the subject of planting, plant a tree! This is another great way to make a difference for future generations. A tree planted will stand for many generations to come and you will have done something that will continue to help the planet long after you have left it.

Because so many trees are cut down every day, there is no such thing as planting too many trees. Everyone on earth would have to plant at least three trees a day to replace the trees that are destroyed in the rainforests by developers. Since it's impossible for everyone to plant three trees a day, we can help in other ways, such as reducing the need to cut down so many trees.

"Going paperless" is an excellent way to reduce the need to cut down more and more trees. Most companies offer online billing and banks can give you your monthly bank statements through e-mail. You can even pay your bills online through the company's website with your bank card or online bill pay through your financial institution.

Having your bill payments taken directly out of your checking or savings account each and every month eliminates the need for mailing envelopes, both sent to you and sent by you. It will also save you money on postage by not having to buy as many stamps. Also, it will avoid your having to make a trip to the post office, saving gas and helping reduce air pollution.

While you're at the store and looking at the boxes anyway, try to buy products that are packaged in one hundred percent recycled materials. You will be shocked to find out that nearly everything you buy can be purchased in recycled containers.

Getting your children involved in your efforts will help them develop their own passion for wildlife protection. Have them spend less time playing video games and more time outside enjoying the outdoors and every advantage it has to offer.

If staying indoors is more appealing to them, have them watch television programs that will peak their interest with wildlife such as the Discovery Channel and Animal Planet. Watching shows such as The Crocodile Hunter, Bindi the Jungle Girl, The Jeff Corwin Experience and related programs can educate them on the importance of conservation and instill a lifelong desire to help the environment. There are also thousands of books they can read that teach about animals and how to protect them.

One game I have made up for my children to play is at the beginning of the week, each of my kids can pick an animal, any animal, and then spend all week learning about the animal they chose. At the end of the week, we have a contest to see who learned the most about their animal. Whoever learned the most gets a reward. You would not believe how excited a child can get about learning! And not only do they learn about the animal they have been studying, they learn about the animals that the other children were studying about from their sharing about them at the end of the week. Win, win!

Using the same concept, you can choose to use

plants instead of animals. Or different countries that animals live in or what kind of habitat they require. By making a variety of choices in variations, you are keeping it interesting and the children will never become bored with this game, or run out of things to learn about.

Nobody expects any one person to do everything suggested in this chapter. If you can, then good on you! If not, scan through all of the options listed and pick out a few things that you know you will be able to follow through with. Even think for yourself of some other things you can do that aren't mentioned here. The point is to make a realistic plan and then just go for it!!!

SPECIAL THANKS

To thank all of the people who helped me in my quest to write this book and pay my respects to the entire Irwin family would be a book all on it's own. There are, however, a few people that without their help, encouragement and all around perseverance, I would not have had the strength or courage to continue writing.

First, of course, I would like to thank my family.

My husband, Greg Guthrie, for being so understanding and supportive when I had no experience in writing. My mother, Pat Mosher, for always backing me up. Whether you thought I could do something or not, you always encouraged me to continue forward with any dream or crazy scheme I had.

My children, Randi Bekstrom, Gary, Karen, Jenee, CJ, Jillian and Mandy Guthrie. You are my angels and my pride and joy. I thank God everyday for putting each and every one of you in my life. I know that writing this book has taken a lot of time away from all of you and I thank you for understanding why it was so important for me to continue so diligently.

Other family that have been so important to me throughout my life and who were there for me during my venture down that road to self discovery include my brothers, Jim and Mike Danich, my sister, Yvonne Abbott, my brother-in law, Ralph Abbott, my sister-in-law, Monica Danich, my nieces, Amber Bailey, Megan Abbott and Tiffany Danich, my nephews, Mike Jr. and Nick Danich.

Then there are those who have been an important part of my life, whose influences has helped me become the person I am today and are still very important to me in every way. They include Mike Bekstrom, Norma and Gus Bekstrom, Cathy Sue Bekstrom, Stacy Kelly, Gary and Susie Kelly, Chris and Greg Kelly, Marty Barnett, Matthew Barnett, Steve Barnett, Sharon and Clay Barnett, Eddie Blanco, Jack Fox, Leslie Shean, Russ Crowley, David Jones, Melinda Smith, Julie Cummings-Stoller, Debbie and Cesar Ortiz, Pastor Bayless Connelly, Pastor Paul Stumpf, Pastor Steve Daily, Bob and Evie Johnson, John Belcher and Karen Keck, Tony and Belinda Garcia, Rob and Cathy Doran, Johnny and Donna Hayes, Dina and Canera Miles, Rose and Hector Flores, Deborah Johnson, Bob Reynolds, John Schildroth, Jack Grisham, Karsten Reynolds, Ladonna Godbehere, Tim Godbehere, Carson Lowe, everyone at Colton Community Church, Cottonwood Christian Center and Celebration Center.

Special recognition to those my children refer to as their guardian angels. They are Edmund Montgomery, Leslie Tighe, Luvia Zepeda and Annette Jenkins.

I would also like to thank the Discovery Channel and Animal Planet for taking a leap of faith and bringing so much joy and education to millions of people all over the world.

Thank you, Steve Irwin. Along with millions of others, you gave me something that I have never had before, a purpose and a passion. You are my hero.

BIBLIOGRAPHY

There were many books, videos and web sites that I used as reference when I began this book. Below is a list of some of them, the ones I used as references to names, dates and a few sporadic events. Most of what I wrote in this book was from memory, what I had heard and seen for myself over a span of 10 years. For those, I can only give credit to Steve and Terri Irwin, Bob and Lyn Irwin, Bindi and Robert Irwin, Wes Mannion, John Stainton, The Discovery Channel, Animal Planet and the entire Australia Zoo.

"Steve & Me" by Terri Irwin, © 2007, "The Crocodile Hunter" by Steve and Terri Irwin, © 1998
www.wildlifewarriors.org, www.australiazoo.com.au,
www.biography.com, www.animal.discovery.com,
www.ozmagic.homestead.com, www.crochunter.com.au,
www.wikipedia.com, www.wikiquote.com,
www.environment.about.com, www.shamozzle.com,
www.mediaman.com.au, www.newsgab.com,
www.answers.com, www.goaustralia.about.com,
www.theage.com.au, www.outsidethebeltway.com
"He Changed Our World: Steve Irwin Memorial Tribute" © 2006,
"Ocean's Deadliest" © 2006, "The Crocodile Hunter: Collision Course" © 2002
"The Crocodile Hunter" - Animal Planet
"The Crocodile Hunter Diaries" - Animal Planet
"Croc Files" - Animal Planet
"Bindi the Jungle Girl" - Discovery Kids
"20/20" with Barbara Walters - Terri Irwin Interview
CNN News Broadcast
Los Angeles Times, The San Bernardino Sun, New York Times, People & Time Magazines